Oily Cart
all sorts of theatre for all sorts of kids

all sorts of theatre for all sorts of kids

*Compiled and edited
by Mark Brown*

Trentham Books

Stoke on Trent, UK and Sterling , USA

Trentham Books Limited
Westview House   22883 Quicksilver Drive
734 London Road   Sterling
Oakhill   VA 20166-2012
Stoke on Trent   USA
Staffordshire
England ST4 5NP

First published 2012

British Library Cataloguing-in-Publication Data
A catalogue record for this book is available from the
British Library

Photos: amanda@oliycart.org.uk

ISBN 978-1-85856-510-1

Designed and typeset by Trentham Books Ltd, Chester
Printed and bound in Great Britain by 4edge Limited, Hockley

Contents

CONTENTS

Acknowledgements

The editor would like to offer the following thanks to those who assisted in bringing this book together

One look at the contents pages of this book offers abundant evidence that it is, like the work of Oily Cart itself, very much a collective effort. Most of those who require my thanks – from the essayists and the interviewees, to the critics who have contributed reviews to the book – are named in the pages that follow. However, there are a number of others who deserve my gratitude and acknowledgement.

Roger Lang (general manager of Oily Cart) and Alison Garratt (the company's administrator) have, alongside the core members of the company themselves, made a crucial contribution in a number of key areas; from locating archive material to furnishing me with information about Oily Cart shows past that it would, otherwise, have been nigh on impossible for me to locate. Alan Morrison, my arts editor at the *Sunday Herald*, must be thanked for delving into the paper's archives in order that I could be sure of the date of publication of my review of *Conference of the Birds*. Thanks are due to my family – my partner, Nicole Brodie, and my children Cara and Ethan – for their tremendous patience as I laboured over the more unglamorous aspects of editing.

Thanks are due to Gillian Klein at Trentham Books, who has been both an immensely patient and a gratifyingly engaged editor, in the face of the numerous delays and changes that Oily Cart and I have imposed upon her.

Finally, my warmest thanks to the creative core of Oily Cart – Tim Webb, Claire de Loon and Max Reinhardt – for the huge contributions they have made, as writers, interviewees and the most wonderfully involved of interested parties, throughout the process of this book's creation. While I take full responsibility for any errors that might occur within the volume, insofar as it conveys something of the essence of Oily Cart as a theatre company, this book belongs, first and foremost, to them.

Foreword
Oily Cart – into Wonderland
Lyn Gardner

There are good theatre companies, and there are great theatre companies. There are great theatre companies, and there is Oily Cart. I'm reminded of that every time I go and see the company's work because they never fail to surprise me. An Oily Cart show is like falling down a rabbit hole and finding yourself in Wonderland. Every show is an adventure – sometimes awe-inspiring, sometimes self-reflective, sometimes a little bit scary – that makes you look both at the world and theatre itself anew.

On occasion an Oily Cart show will mean sitting in a theatre watching children move the story on, as in the wonderfully tactile *Ring a Ding Ding*, a performance in which the children must help the stage rotate so that the story can develop. Or it could mean donning a swimming costume and plunging into a swimming pool in a school in South London for *Pool Piece*, a one-on-one show that is immersive in every way. In a show like *Something in the Air*, you could find yourself suspended, bouncing and swinging on a flower-covered seat high above the ground as you watch the cast swoop through the air like exotic birds and feel as if you are taking flight and flying too.

Of course to talk of seeing or watching Oily Cart's multisensory, interactive work doesn't even begin to scratch the surface of a theatre experience that is often as much about smelling, hearing, touching and feeling a rush of fanned air against your face as it is about seeing in any traditional theatre context. Oily Cart audiences are not just spectators, they are participants too. In 2010's *Mole in the Hole* audiences really did scratch about as we felt and heard the crunch of dry leaves under our feet and followed the glittering snail trail through the forest and down the mole hole into the dark, aided by the faint glow of helpful glow worms.

Thirty years since it was founded to create theatre for young audiences, Oily Cart still has its wheels on track. It is not just a key player in the grossly under-valued Cinderella sector of children's theatre, where superb companies such as Fevered Sleep, Theatre-Rites and artists such as Mark Storrer also go un-sung and under-appreciated. Like those very best companies working with children, it is a pioneer on the wider stage of contemporary UK theatre. What is it that sets a great theatre company apart from the merely good? It is, of course, the ability to produce high quality work over a long period of time, but I believe that it is also about openness and innovation. Through a 30-year body of work, Oily Cart has consistently asked questions about theatrical form, the way in which narrative is used and how the rules of spectatorial engagement can be mischievously adapted and changed for the benefit of young audiences and their carers. For three decades the company has been investigating the very nature of theatre itself. Every new show is a question, not an answer.

Long before the current passion for immersive and site-specific theatre and one-on-one festivals, created by companies such as Punchdrunk and venues such as Battersea Arts Centre, Oily Cart was creating complete, installation-style environments out of the most unpromising spaces: a school dinner hall smelling faintly of cabbage is transformed into an Aladdin's cave with a ceil-ing full of stars and the wafting smells of lavender and spice; an echoing, chlorine-reeking swimming pool becomes an exotic watery playground with strange, bobbing Heath Robinson-ish contraptions.

While many immersive companies making work for adult audiences will search for months, sometimes even years, to find the perfect unoccupied warehouse or derelict space for their show, Oily Cart, touring to school halls and black-box theatre spaces, must simply rise to the challenge of working with what is available to them. With the economic climate for the arts growing ever more chilly, their make do and mend attitude may well offer a useful lesson to others.

It is obvious, too, that the company's 30-year-old DIY aesthetic – born from the early days when necessity was very much the mother of invention for designer Claire de Loon – is currently becoming wildly fashionable amongst a rising generation of theatre makers, including companies such as Little Bulb, Action Hero and Rash Dash, who also find themselves making theatre in an age of austerity. It often feels that where Oily Cart have led, others will eventually follow.

What makes the company a trailblazer is that it has never been derailed from its mission to create superb theatre for children of all ages and situations, including babies and children with profound and multiple learning difficulties or autistic spectrum disorder. However, it has also demonstrated a rare talent for creative renewal and experiment with the entire range of tools in the theatrical palette, and always learned from its past experiments. Ten years on from *Big Splash*, the first of the company's hydrotherapy pools shows, Oily Cart demonstrated in *Pool Piece* all the lessons learned from that early experiment in a show in which soundscape, sensory diversions, colour and water came together in a liquid world of enchantment.

Oily Cart has turned what many theatre companies would regard as insurmountable challenges-creating shows for children who are often either pre-verbal or non-verbal, who have short attention spans and don't like sitting still for too long-into positives. These positives have led to the development of work that has always naturally done what many 21st-century theatre companies are now striving to do: namely, attempting to grapple with fast-moving cultural shifts that increasingly suggest that audiences do not just want theatre made for them, but are eager for theatre experiences that are made with them.

Over the last ten years the UK's theatre culture has perhaps been more fluid than at any time since the 60s and more open to the new and the experimental. There are puppets in the West End with *War Horse*. A giant mechanical elephant takes over the streets of London; a massive spider stops the traffic in Liverpool. 1927's The Animals and Children Took to the Streets is invited to the National Theatre. Much of this work reflects the massive shifts taking place in the relationship between theatre and audiences. Just as the relationship of publishers to readers or music makers to listeners, has changed dramatically over the last few years because of the rise of digital technologies, so those cultural changes are affecting the long-established relationship between theatre and theatre audiences.

Just as the age of the CD is over-transformed by technological advances that mean that teenagers can make albums in their own bedroom and also download the work of artists they like at the touch of a screen – so, the age of the theatre as a product to be consumed is in retreat. This does not mean that there will be no new plays by Tom Stoppard watched by audiences sitting in neat rows in 19th-century playhouses, and no stadium shows of Fireman Sam, Peppa Pig and other popular children's TV characters. Of course there will be. But it does also mean that more radical forms, in particular the theatre of participation, are on the rise. Audiences are hungry for different kinds of theatre experience, and that often means interactive experiences.

Theatre of participation only happens where we, as members of the audience, have an active engagement in the work – when it genuinely matters that we are there in the space with the performers. It gives us the freedom to act, not just to be acted upon. Its fast-growing appeal is demonstrated in the increasing popularity of work from companies such as Coney, and Hide and Seek, who often use the narrative techniques and models of computer games and who give audiences the sense of being inside a game, the outcomes of which can be influenced by the behaviour of the players.

Oily Cart understood the need to make this shift for their audiences long before digital technologies and pervasive media transformed all our everyday lives and the way we work, play, communicate and share. By its very nature, Oily Cart's work has always been participatory and always acutely attuned to the relationship between performer and audience. How could it not be, having found such success with audiences most of whom have never heard of the fourth wall and wouldn't give a fig for it if they had? Audiences whose daily experience is often on the margins of life and society, either through age or disability, but who, through the work of Oily Cart, get the opportunity to be part of an unfolding performance. Audiences who may not be able to sit, but may need to lie or be in a harness and who may emit voluntary and involuntary sounds throughout the performance or even have a quick nap.

The shows have to be able to accommodate them all, and in accommodating them Oily Cart has developed a practice that is inclusive, audience-centred and, therefore, often theatrically radical in the way the relationship of spectators to the work plays out. Our presence really does matter. In *Blue* – a piece inspired by the smoky, bluesy music of the Mississippi Delta and beyond, which curls like a memory through your brain – the show began with the audience offering up their own 'blues boxes' of precious memories and objects for everyone to share. When the company goes into schools it is often not for a flash and dash performance; rather, the show will be a culmination of a period spent working with students in the school. When I've been to see Oily Cart's work *in situ*, the atmosphere is often that of a fete or holiday. Wheelchairs are decorated in a way that reflects the theme of the show, and the children are already familiar with the characters who may well have been embedded in the school and working with them over a period of time. The work is not just made and distributed, it is shared on every level.

The show can never go on without us. We are encouraged to play within the play, and depending on our reaction it may expand to incorporate us. Many years ago, I saw a performance of a show called *Over the Moon*, in which a profoundly deaf little boy kept trying to touch and climb into a tuba, clearly enticed by the vibrations. Because it was an Oily Cart show he was encouraged in his endeavour, not repulsed. In Oily Cart shows there is no need for the fourth wall to be broken wide open, it simply isn't there in the first place; there is no barrier between us and them.

Words may often play second fiddle to visuals, sound and sensory input, but that is not to say that narrative and meaning is neglected in an Oily Cart performance. The audience are invited to be collaborators. Shows are always open, never closed, in their narratives and they may offer up not just one meaning but many. Just as the company is innovative in the way it uses physical space, so it is always generous, too, in the way it allows space within the storytelling for the audience to bring their own imagination and experience to bear, whatever our age or cognitive ability. We are actively involved all along the way.

Ring a Ding Ding may be read as an absurdist fantasy, a shaggy dog story, or existential meditation of our smallness in the vastness of the universe, but we can all take from it what we most need from it at the moment we experience it. It can mean what we need it to mean for us as it works its sly theatrical magic, acts upon us and we act upon it. In that moment of alchemy, the experience begins to affect and change us. Every Oily Cart show makes it explicit that this is one company for whom audiences – whatever their age – are not an inconvenient necessity, but crucial collaborators in the quest to interrogate theatre and discover the best it can and might be in the 21st-century.

Lyn Gardner writes about theatre and performance for the Guardian, *and is the author of several novels for children.*

A note on the editor

Mark Brown is theatre critic of the Scottish national newspaper the *Sunday Herald* and a theatre and performing arts critic for the UK newspaper the *Daily Telegraph*. He teaches theatre studies and theatre criticism at the Royal Conservatoire of Scotland. He is a member of the executive committee of the International Association of Theatre Critics, for which he is also adjunct director of young critics' seminars. He is a member of the editorial board of the IATC's webjournal Critical Stages and English-language supervisor for the theatre webjournal *Prospero European Review*. He is editor of the book *Howard Barker Interviews 1980-2010: Conversations in Catastrophe* (published by Intellect Books). In 1999 he received the Edinburgh Festival Fringe Society's Allen Wright Award for outstanding arts journalism by a young writer.

Introduction
Mark Brown

The idea for this book came about as Oily Cart celebrated its 30th ainniversary in 2011. It was a remarkable milestone for a theatre company that had its roots in a chance meeting between Tim Webb and Claire de Loon (who would later become husband and wife) at the Citizens Theatre in Glasgow in 1971 and a further chance meeting between them and Max Reinhardt at the Battersea Arts Centre in London in 1977. The common passion and commitment that they discovered for making theatre of the highest quality for some of the most neglected audiences (namely, very young children and children and young adults with often complex learning disabilities) would lead them to create a theatre company that, it is no exaggeration to say, has revolutionised work in its chosen fields over the past three decades.

While this book is a celebration of 30 years of Oily Cart, it also has other objectives. Firstly, through a series of essays by the founders of the company themselves, it seeks to provide the reader with a sense of the history and development of Oily Cart.

Secondly, this volume aims to act as a guide to how Oily Cart approaches work for its various audiences. To that end the book is constructed around five distinct sections, namely:

1) Pieces by Tim Webb, Claire de Loon and Max Reinhardt, the three artists who constitute the creative core of Oily Cart, exploring how the company's shows are created from the directorial, design and musical perspectives.

2) A detailed focus upon three Oily Cart shows: *Blue, Baby Balloon* and *Ring a Ding Ding*. These shows come from Oily Cart's work for three distinct audiences: firstly, children and young adults with learning disabilities; secondly, babies and toddlers; and finally, children aged two and over. The

three shows, and the similarities and differences in the company's approach to staging them, are considered from various perspectives. This section of the book also includes the full script of *Blue*, which offers readers a tremendous window into the Oily Cart method.

3) In the third section, entitled 'The Casts', six performers talk to me about working with Oily Cart. The interviews focus upon specific shows across the range of the company's work. They also invite the performers to reflect upon the unique experiences gained by those who perform with the company.

4) In 'Perspectives on Oily Cart' we see the company as others see them. From a fellow theatre maker, to academic researchers, professional theatre critics and the views of various audience members, particularly the relatives, teachers and carers of children who have experienced Oily Cart's work, this section offers a rich and diverse set of responses to the company's performances.

5) Finally, in the section entitled 'The Real Nitty Gritty', Claire de Loon and Tim Webb deal, respectively, with the technical and administrative work that, although usually hidden and uncelebrated, is absolutely essential to sustaining Oily Cart as a theatre company.

So this book is a celebratory collection and overview for: anyone who has ever seen and loved the work of Oily Cart; anyone who makes or would like to make theatre for young children or children and young adults with learning disabilities; anyone who teaches people with special educational needs or young children; anyone who is interested in drama therapy or music therapy.

It is also a book for anyone who simply wants to know how and why one of Britain's finest theatre companies does what it does.

The History of Oily Cart
Tim Webb

I n 1977 Claire de Loon, Max Reinhardt and I first met up at Battersea Arts Centre. But for that fateful encounter there would've been no Oily Cart.

Claire and I actually got together when we were working at the Glasgow Citizens Theatre back in 1971. Claire was an assistant designer, I was in my first job as an assistant stage manager. Claire went on to design a number of productions at the Citizens and then was designer for an array of rep, fringe and Theatre-in-Education (TIE) companies, including a stint as head of design at Crewe. Meanwhile I became a performer and writer with the Citizens TIE company and then with Greenwich Young People's Theatre, another TIE team. I also spent two years in rep as assistant director at the New Victoria Theatre, Stoke-on-Trent, a theatre-in-the-round where I probably got my taste for different ways of staging.

Tim in Picnic 1985. Photo: Brian Campbell

By 1977 Claire had become the organiser of the activities for children at Battersea Arts Centre. Here she encountered Max Reinhardt, also based at the centre, who was the head of the Inner London Education Authority Family Workshop Unit. This progressive outfit programmed educational and cultural activities for family groups, with adults and children participating together. Max had had experience in alternative education, both in this country and in Canada, but wanted to become more involved with music, something he'd neglected since a chequered career in university bands. We decided to work together, though the beginning was very modest.

For several years I'd been trying to master the Punch and Judy man's 'swazzle', the device that fits in the puppeteer's mouth to give the authentic sound of Punch's voice. Unfortunately it gave me the authentic sound of someone choking. Max volunteered to stand in front of the puppet booth, singing and saying things like, 'What's that Mr Punch? You think you saw the Policeman?' to accompany the gagging sounds from within.

Before long Max and I began to have doubts about Punch as an entertainment for the very young children who seemed to comprise the majority of our audiences. A highlight of our Punch was when the Policeman went to investigate the Sausage Machine, and emerged as a string of (blue) sausages. We thought that we could make something more appropriate for the under-fives.

I had had some experience of theatre for the under-fives when working in TIE, and both Max and myself had worked with the pioneering company Theatre Kit, one of the first in the UK to consistently make theatre for the very young.

In October, 1981, with a budget of £40, we made *Out of Their Tree*, specifically for children from three to five years of age. It was quite a success. Max and I took the plunge and began full-time work as Oily Cart.

We found that by combining a variety of theatrical languages, including strong visuals, puppetry and live music, we could hold an audience of under-fives for 45 minutes or more. Our shows for this age range would start off in a situation familiar to the children – such as a kitchen, a picnic or a bus trip. However, they would then spiral off into fantastical developments; such as, for example, when the goldfish that was won at the funfair turned out to be a baby whale (*Soapsuds*, 1985).

Back in the Punch and Judy days, we had discovered that under-fives have little time for the concept of the fourth wall in theatre. If something interesting was happening in front of them, then they wanted to talk to the characters, even get up on stage and physically help out. In our turn, we were happy to provide plenty of opportunities for their direct participation in a world increasingly filled with digital entertainments.

In the Oily Cart's second year we made *Prehistoric Playtime* (1982), our first show for seven to eleven-year-olds. Our shows for the older children had the same variety of visuals and live music as the work for the very young but had, inevitably, more complex narratives and more verbal language. Although many of these productions had themes that might be explored later in the classroom, such as the treatment of piracy and the slave trade in *Parrots of Penzance* (1984), our main goal was to be theatrical not educational. Certainly some of the topics dealt with in our shows, for example, the role played by space aliens in the disappearance of Atlantis, in *The Bermuda Rectangle* (1987), are unlikely to feature on the National Curriculum.

In 1984 we received our first subsidy, a grant from the Greater London Council's Arts Committee that enabled us to add a black performer, Fay Roach, to the company. We'd become increasingly aware that a company of two prematurely balding white males did not reflect the composition of our audiences. Since then we have always tried to have a company on stage that related to the gender and ethnic make-up of the young people watching the shows.

In those early days we relied on box office and were rebuffed more than once when we approached the Arts Council of Great Britain. How well I remember an official telling us that a report on our first show found it 'simply appalling'. Happy days. But then in 1990, we were given revenue funding from the Arts Council and we are delighted that this support has continued until the present day.

Back in the seventies I had been involved in a Glasgow Citizens TIE team production for Special Needs schools. So when in 1988, a school for young people with severe learning disabilities wanted to book one of our under-fives shows for its three to eighteen-year-old students, we asked if we could rather work with the school to develop a more age-appropriate show. Talking to the staff and playing with the students, we found the school contained an enormous range of abilities. Some of the older students were both highly verbal and mobile. On the other hand there were young people with complex sensory and intellectual disabilities who needed assistance with most everyday activities. Of course, there were also a great number of young people between these two extremes and we saw that no one form of theatre was going to satisfy the requirements of everyone in the school.

Two other discoveries made in that school have informed our work for this sector ever since. First, staff members made it clear that we needed to spend a good deal longer with the young people in the school than the usual 45-50 minute show. The students needed more time to get to know us, and we needed more time to tune into them. So our first Special Needs schools show, *Box of Socks* (1988), took place over a whole school day. A trio of aliens from outer space crashed their spaceship into the morning assembly and spent the rest of the day wandering all over the school, baffled by life on Earth. This turned out to be an empowering event for the school students who had to explain aspects of human behaviour, from eating to writing, to the extraplanetary visitors.

Our other discovery was the kinaesthetic sense: the sense that the body has of its position and movement. In the school there was much use of a technique called 'hammocking', in which staff members would swing a participant in a navy hammock. The process clearly gave much pleasure to the young people, and especially to those with impaired vision or hearing.

From 1988 to the present day, Oily Cart has toured at least one production for these audiences with severe learning disabilities each year. Up until 1996 our programmes often spent two days in each school visited and would try to provide something for everyone in the school. There would be a range of modules pitched at different ability levels, as well as opening and closing moments when the whole school would be brought together.

For example, for *Georgie Goes to Hollywood* (1994) we had created, in the rehearsal period, the opening and closing footage of an adventure video. During our two days in the schools we shot the other scenes for the film during the different modules. Many of the students had roles to play. But there was also a sequence that involved the young people with multiple impairments and minimal verbal language, the group often labelled as having profound and multiple learning disabilities (PMLD). This sequence was videoed and incorporated into the final presentation but it could also be enjoyed, in the moment, as a series of sensory events. At the end of the two days the whole school would dress up for the world premiere of the film they had created.

In 1996 we were invited to take up residence in Smallwood School in Wandsworth. It's invaluable for us to have all branches of the company on one site and I believe that having a children's theatre company, which combines so many art forms, on site provides a rich resource for the school as well as a testing ground for our new shows. We have been in Smallwood – where we have space for workshops, an office and a rehearsal room – ever since and so continue to remain in Wandsworth, the borough where the company began and that has done so much to support us over the years.

As we worked more and more in Special Needs schools during the nineties, we came to realise that the young people with PMLD not only showed some astonishing reactions to our work, but also had the least alternative cultural provision. So, in 1996, we created our first piece, *Tickled Pink*, specifically for them. From then on all our work in Special Needs schools has been much more tightly focused, and nowadays we concentrate on young people labelled as having profound and multiple learning disabilities or an autistic spectrum disorder (ASD).

We know that this kind of theatre has to be multisensory, addressing all the senses, not just those theatre stand-bys, seeing and hearing. Our performances may involve aromatherapy, hand and foot massage, fans and foam, as well as characters who are identified by the texture or the scents of their costumes, and the iconic props they carry. A very significant role in this side of the Oily Cart's work has been played by a charismatic, deep-voiced Mark Foster who himself has a learning disability. Mark has done much more than bring his own remarkable presence and empathy to our performances; he has enabled us to see something of the community of people with learning disabilities through his eyes, and so help transform the ethos of the company.

Nowadays we pay a good deal of attention to the kinaesthetic sense, the sense that the body has of its own position and movement in space. Our attention had originally been drawn to this sense by the use of hammocking in the school where we prepared our first Special Needs school show. In 1999 we developed an alternative way of engaging the kinaesthetic sense by working in hydrotherapy pools.

In the pools, participants are freed from the constraints of wheelchairs, braces and splints in which many of them have to spend their lives. Additionally, the working relationship between performer and participant is particularly good in the water, where the two are face to face for much of the time.

In pursuit of the kinaesthetic sense we made our first trampoline-based show, Boing, in 2002 and found that, as with the water shows, the trampoline allowed many of the participants a much wider than usual range of movement. Our trampoline productions also saw the increasing involvement of people with an autistic spectrum disorder. The schools told us that many on the spectrum were fascinated by trampoline and other g-force inducing, kinaesthetically intense activities.

For our second trampoline show, *Moving Pictures* (2003), we introduced large-scale live video projection to enable the participants to locate themselves more firmly at the centre of the action,

In *Something in the Air* (2009-2012), made with Ockham's Razor, the brilliant aerial company, and originally a commission from the Manchester International Festival, we explored the kinaesthetic sense by hoisting the whole audience, six young people with six companions, into the air in specially designed seating, where they could swing, bounce and spin, mirroring the aerialists who fly above, besides and below them.

As well as being multisensory, we also know that our theatre for young people with complex learning disabilities has to be highly interactive. For example, in *Something in the Air*, one young person will want to be high, while another will prefer to stay low; one participant will want to bounce while another prefers to sway. As we work in a very close-up way, with relatively small audiences, we are able to scrutinise the reactions of the young people, and their adult companions and adapt what we are doing to individual responses. The Oily Cart has to watch the audience members far more intently than they watch us.

In all of our theatre for those with complex learning disabilities, and especially those on the autism spectrum, we have found that preparation in advance of a performance is beneficial for the participants. Nowadays we invariably make a 'social story', which helps our audience engage with the production. We came across the 'social story' concept in Special Needs schools, where it is often used to help young people on the autism spectrum, who commonly have difficulties with social interaction. A 'social story' explains in clear terms, using graphics, the accepted behaviour involved in, for example, eating in public or visiting a grandparent. We use the 'social story' to introduce the characters in a show, the setting where it will take place, and the seats the audience will be using. The stories will also suggest ways in which the participants can prepare for the performance experience, for example, by making something that will be used in the show and how they might respond to the characters. For example: 'It's okay to laugh,' and 'You can say 'okay' if you would like to do this, or 'no' if you'd rather not.'

One huge advantage of our form of theatre for participants on the spectrum is that in a performance they will be involved in an experience that is distilled so that the chance of sensory overload is reduced, and which is ordered and predictable. Armed with a social story and a timeline, a graphic illustration of the sequence of events in a show, the participants can see where they are up to in a performance and anticipate the ending. Theatre is, after all, usually more predictable than life.

But while the demystification of the theatre process is a significant part of the Oily Cart strategy, we sometimes adopt a completely different approach. As part of the preparations for Special Needs schools shows we sometimes embed a character from a production in the schools for several days before the performances. At first these characters have little to do with the young people, which builds curiosity, and soon many of the students want to find out all about the character and to tell him or her all about their lives and school activities.

Our social stories are available as DVDs, as photo-illustrated stories that can be downloaded from our web site and as hard copies. In addition, staff briefing sessions often form part of an Oily Cart visit to a school. These briefing sessions and social stories also suggest to staff and parents ways in which the immense stimulus of a theatre experience can be followed up, with ideas for practical activities back in the home or the classroom. At best our theatre begins long before the participants encounter a live actor, and continues to motivate activity long after the performance has finished.

It took us rather a long time to realise that the multisensory, close-up, highly interactive form of theatre we had devised for young people with complex disabilities might be relevant to other audiences. In fact it wasn't until 2001 that we began to create theatre for children from six months to two years old, as part of our production, *Jumpin' Beans*. The under-twos are another audience that is primarily non-verbal – perhaps I should say pre-verbal – who know little and care less about theatrical conventions and are often as much interested in smelling and tasting new phenomena, including performers, as they are in looking at or listening to them. Of course, in many other ways these two audiences could not be more different. I am still astounded by the intense focus and speed of response of a neurotypical audience of babies and toddlers. In 2004 we made another piece, *Hippity Hop*, 'the world's first hip hop musical for babies and toddlers', though this show also existed in a version for two to four-year-olds. At last, with *Baby Balloon* in 2006, we created our first production solely for children under two. This was a very well received piece, featuring the projection of video of the children's faces onto balloons and an invitation to the audience to join us inside a very large balloon, an inflatable, where we all ate tangerines, making a wonderful miasma.

And now it's 2012, amazingly our 30th year. We currently have *Ring A Ding Ding*, a studio theatre show for three to six-year-olds on tour after a four-week Christmas run at the Unicorn. Later in the year we'll be touring *Drum*, a show for under-twos, with versions for young people with complex disabilities or on the autistic spectrum, to Abu Dhabi. From April to May we'll be re-touring *Something In the Air*, and in May we will be opening *In a Pickle*, a co-production with the Royal Shakespeare Company that reimagines Shakespeare's *The Winter's Tale* for two to four-year-olds. This mix of the three types of Oily production is typical of our annual touring pattern and is likely to continue for the foreseeable future – but that, of course, is another story.

I am aware of two major omissions in this gallop through the Oily Cart's history. Firstly, I have hardly mentioned any of the amazing performers, who have actually done so much to create the shows and then deliver them out there in the schools and theatres. I'm going to be invidious and single out Geoff Bowyer, Jonny Quick and Carol Walton from the early days; and Ruth Calkin, Nicole Worrica, Patrick Lynch, Sjaak van der Bent, Griff Fender and the one and only Mark Foster from later versions of the company.

Secondly, I've said nothing about the business side of the Oily Cart, without which there would be no shows. We've been blessed with some wonderful general managers and administrators, but they must be the subject of another chapter.

The Oily Cart timeline

The following timeline details all of Oily Cart's shows

❶ Age 6 months to 2 years

❷ Age 2 to 5 years

❸ Age 3 to 6 years

❹ Age 5 to 9 years

❺ Age 7 to 11 years

❻ Young people with severe learning difficulties

❼ Young people with profound and multiple learning disabilities

❽ Young people with complex disabilities and/or an autistic spectrum disorder

* denotes 1 whole day per performance

** denotes 2 whole days per performance

1971 *Tim Webb and Claire de Loon meet for the first time at the Citizens Theatre in Glasgow*

1977 *Tim and Claire meet Max Reinhardt for the first time at Battersea Arts Centre*

1981 Exploding Punch and Judy❷; Out of Their Tree❷

1982 Prehistoric Playtime❺; Bus Stop❷; Grease❺; Bats in Their Belfry❺

1983 Rainbow Robbers❷; Beam Us Up Spotty❺; Bedtime Story❷

1984 Parrots of Penzance❺; Seaside (*first show with three in the cast, thanks to grant from the Greater London Council*)❷; Down the Plughole❹

1985 Picnic❷; Tibet or Not Tibet❺; Soapsuds❷

1986   Slipped Disco❺; Up On the Roof❷

1987   Curse of the Mummy's Sphinx❺; Box of Tricks❷; Bermuda Rectangle❺

1988   *Box of Socks (*first show for young people with Severe Learning Disabilities*)❻; Playhouse❷

1989   *Pleasuredome❻; Chest of Drawers❷

1990   *Company first receives Arts Council of Great Britain revenue funding*
*Colour Me Colour You❻; Ocean Notion❺; Red Lorry Yellow Lorry❷; Will It Hurt?❸

1991   *Funky Philharmonic❻; Off the Wall❷; It Crept from the Crypt❺

1992   *Dinner Ladies from Outer Space❻; Greenfingers❷; Gobble and Gook❹

1993   **EuroBroadbent (*first show to spend two days in each school it visited*)❻; A Bit Missing❷; Fishing for Pigs❸

1994   **Georgie Goes To Hollywood❻; A Peck of Pickled Pepper❷

1995   **George After a Fashion❻; Perfect Present❷

1996   *Tickled Pink (*first show for young people with profound and multiple learning disabilities*)❼; **George Sells Out❻; Roly Poly Pudding❷

1997   *Over The Moon❼; Bubbles! (first water show)❼; A Peck of Pickled Pepper (*first Wonderland installation show*)❷

1998   Hunky Dory!❼; Pass the Parcel❷

1999   Big Splash!❼; **Play House (*performance with installation*)❷

2000   Dreams and Secrets❼; Knock! Knock! Who's There?❷

2001   Waving❼; **Under Your Hat (*performance with installation*)❸

2002   Boing! (*first trampoline show*)❼; Jumpin' Beans (*first show for six months to two-year-olds*)❶❷❸

2003   Moving Pictures (*first show to use live video*)❼; Baking Time (*co-production with Carousel Players, Canada*)❷

2004   Conference of the Birds (*first show for young people with an autistic spectrum disorder*)❽; The Genie's Lamp and the Ship of Gold (*outdoor event with inflatables and fountains*)❷; Hippity Hop (*co-production with Lyric Hammersmith*)❶❷

2005   Conference of the Birds❽; King Neptune and the Pirate Queen (*outdoor event with inflatables and fountains*)❷; If All the World Were Paper❸

2006   Baby Balloon (*co-production with Pantalone, Belgium*)❶; Blue❽; Big Balloon (*co-production with Lyric Hammersmith*)❸

2007   Baby Balloon (*co-production with Pantalone, Belgium*)❶; Blue❽; If All the World Were Paper❸

2008   Baby Balloon (*co-production with Pantalone, Belgium*)❶; Pool Piece❽; How Long is a Piece of String?❸

2009   Something in the Air (*collaboration with Ockham's Razor as part of the Manchester International Festival*)❽; Pool Piece❽; Christmas Baking Time❸

2010   Drum (*baby and toddler version*)❶; Something in the Air❽; Mole in the Hole❸

2011   Drum (*version for children on the autistic spectrum*)❽; Drum (*version for babies and toddlers*)❶; Drum (*version for children with profound and multiple learning disabilities*)❼; Gorgeous (*commission from Manchester International Festival*)❼; Ring a Ding Ding❸

2012   Something in the Air❽; Drum (*co-production with Manchester International Festival, performed at Abu Dhabi Festival*)❶; In a Pickle (*co-production with the RSC for the World Shakespeare Festival*)❷

International Productions of Oily Cart Shows

1998   Roly Poly Pudding – Vulavulani Theatre Company, Soweto, Republic of South Africa

2001/3 Patty's Cake (Peck of Pickled Pepper) – Carousel Players, Ontario, Canada

2003/4 Baking Time – Carousel Players, Ontario, Canada

2007   Red Kite (scratch production) – Chicago Children's Theatre, USA

2008   If All the World Were Paper – Chicago Children's Theatre, USA

2009/10 Blue – EME Foundation/Philharmonie, Luxembourg

The Creative Core

The following pieces – by Oily Cart's artistic director Tim Webb,
head of design Claire de Loon, and musical director Max Reinhardt –
offer in-depth reflections on the company's creative process from
the perspective of each author's particular discipline.

My Life in Cart: writing and directing for Oily Cart
Tim Webb

'm often asked about the creative process of the Oily Cart. I've always thought it so idiosyncratic that I couldn't recommend it as a model for anyone. Still, people will keep asking, so here's my guide to the 'Oily process'.

Stage One: the original idea

Because the Oily Cart makes theatre for several different audiences (for example children under two, or young people on the autism spectrum), new shows tend to evolve differently depending on their target audience. Often a new piece for young people with complex disabilities will be sparked off by some technique we've seen in action in a Special Needs school; for instance, the idea of using suspended seating to make possible a wide range of move-

Tim as Bubbleman in Soapsuds 1985. Photo: Janis Austin

17

ment for the audience in *Something in the Air* (2009-2012) had been stewing away ever since we saw the staff of a Special Needs school rocking the students in hammocks.

Over the years we experimented with rocking chairs, garden swing seats and trampolines before we arrived at the specially constructed seats suspended from a rig on bungee cord in which the *Something in the Air* audiences swing, bounce and spin.

Inspiration can strike in the most unlikely places. Our hydrotherapy pool productions all stemmed from a visit that Claire de Loon and I made to Acton Baths. Half the pool was roped off for an aqua-aerobics class. We thought, 'Ah ha, we know another group of people who'd enjoy something like this.' We knew that many Special Needs schools have hydro pools, and we began to think about a form of water-based theatre for young people with complex learning disabilities.

Of course seeing other people's theatre or, just as often, the work of artists working in other media, has pushed our shows in particular directions. The shadow puppetry that Claire and I saw on a visit to China led to a prolonged use of this medium in Oily shows, and our involvement in the Millenniumjam International Balloon Convention in Belgium helped get our balloon-based shows, *Baby Balloon* and *Big Balloon* air-borne. For Oily Cart travel has always broadened the repertoire.

Sometimes the idea for a show will travel a very long way from its original inspiration. *Blue* (2006), which was made for young people with profound and multiple learning disabilities (PMLD) or an autistic spectrum disorder (ASD), started out as an image of the sort of blue that you see on a video monitor without input. We were in the early stage of work for people on the autism spectrum. With that audience in mind, I wanted to create a minimalist ambience into which we could introduce and withdraw stimuli; one thing, one sound, one colour, one smell at a time, so that each could be appreciated by young people who might be susceptible to sensory overload and certainly need time to process data. Claire asked what sort of music might fit with this blue TV screen image. Why, naturally – the blues. So what are the blues about? Well – sex, death, drink, loneliness, and, curiously, trains. There are an awful lot of blues songs about the railways. From an image of an untuned video screen blue we had arrived at a dramatic situation: what if a show concerned a group of people waiting at a railway station, each with just one piece of luggage? What might those bags and cases contain?

Ideas for new shows have to be fitted into a broad strategy. Nowadays the Oily Cart has a rolling three-year plan, updated three or four times a year, in so-called 'Supabiz' meetings involving the creative team and all full-time staff of the company. The strategy determined in these meetings is very dependent on the agreements we have with Arts Council England and our other major funders, as well as what we simply think would be the most interesting thing to do artistically.

As I write, we are committed to creating two new productions each year – one for very young children, and one for young people with learning disabilities – in addition to touring an established production.

When we start to think about our next show for children under six there are two tactics we often employ. One is to use various materials or processes as the basis for the production. This was the kind of thinking that gave rise to *If All the World Were Paper* (2005 and 2007), in which everything was, or appeared to be, made of paper, and How Long is a Piece of String? (2008), in which everything was string or stringy (though we did make an exception for some lengths of rope). The discipline imposed by making everything in a show from one material, including the music, props and set, drives away the clichés and forces us to be inventive.

The other tactic – and, come to think of it, this is one to which we devote a great deal of time when devising any Oily show whatsoever – is to put ourselves in the shoes of the audience. We try to think as they think and feel as they feel, in order to come up with a story that they will find comprehensible and emotionally engaging. The storyline of How Long is a Piece of String was one that consistently engaged the children. In this show a Heath Robinson-style machine ran amok (a feature of many Oily productions) and produced a crowd of babies made of string – so many, in fact, that there was one for each child in the audience. The children worked out that the best thing to do for these babies was to get them back to their string parents. So, with each child holding a baby, we physically journeyed together in this promenade production through a world of string until the babies were reunited with the string mummy and daddy.

It's important that the themes and the stories of our shows, which absolutely must engage the children – the primary audience – should also interest and entertain the adults, ie the parents, the teachers, the carers and so on, who are invariably present. Firstly, they are actually part of our audience. Why should they not be entertained? Secondly, the reactions of adults in an audience can send large cues to the children present. If the adults are uninterested, then this can inform the reactions of the children. 'Why should I be bothered about this, if Daddy's on the back row reading the paper?' Our strategy for engaging adult audiences these days is simply to make theatre of undeniable quality.

It is true that the language and, to some extent, the themes of our shows are edited to ensure that they are accessible to their intended primary audience, whether that be very young children or young people with complex learning disabilities. That aside, the design, the music, the experimenting with theatrical form, the complexity and intensity of performances and the passion underlying each of our productions should be a rich enough mix for any adult spectator. In the good old days, when it was Max and I performing, our approach was more robust. Many was the Saturday morning we would leave the stage and clamber along the back row of the audience to ask the parents reading the *Guardian* or the *Telegraph* why they preferred that to the theatrical brilliance being dished out at the other end of the room.

Whatever the inspiration, new shows usually first surface as titles with two or three sentences of blurb in our outline three-year plan, some time long before we have any more specific ideas about them. So, by way of example, *Ring a Ding Ding*, our winter 2011-2012 show, was first described in the three-year plan as:

> An immersive, interactive and multisensory piece for an audience of 50-60 – including children 3 to 6, plus their families and friends. The audience will sit around a giant table top, their chins pressed into the surface, the action at eye level. The accompanying family and other adults will sit immediately behind them. The table surface will feature a variety of delightful smells and textures.

Ideas about characters and story came later, as did the theme, which was that this was to be a show about rings: the children would be sitting in a ring; the turntable would revolve; the characters, including a milkman who did his rounds, would go round and round in pursuit of a dog who chased his tail; the music would be based on bell-like ringing instruments; and the set and puppets would make much use of recycled materials.

Stage Two: the script

From such basic beginnings it's my job, working closely with our designer, Claire de Loon, and our music director, Max Reinhardt, to develop the show though a series of scenarios into a script of twenty-odd pages featuring a little dialogue and a great deal of stage direction. Occasionally, as with *Baby Balloon* (2006), there is no sort of script at all, just a list of cues, but the policy is to go into rehearsal with a script.

At the scripting stage we often consult with teachers and other specialists, for example, regarding how the piece might work for people on the autism spectrum. Nowadays we bring together performers and other experts for several development days in which we develop and test concepts before rehearsals begin.

As the script comes together, Claire and I check it to see that we have not neglected any of the factors that we think should be in an Oily Cart show. The most important of these is how the audience will play its part in the performance. When considering a script for children under six who may or may not have disabilities we ask: are there moments when the audience will be able to come through the invisible 'fourth wall' dividing performers from spectators and actually join us in the action? Are there opportunities for the audience to question the characters and make suggestions?

We examine all of our shows, and especially those for young people with PMLD or ASD, to see that they contain other sensory elements beside those old stand-bys of theatre, seeing and hearing. Even after years of creating multisensory productions, it's easy to neglect the other senses, so we check to ensure that an emerging show has things that are good to smell, to touch, perhaps to taste, and that there will be stimulation for the kinaesthetic sense.

We also think very carefully about the totality of our audiences' experience of a show. Elsewhere in this book Claire de Loon explains the various strategies we have for preparing our audiences for their involvement in the performance long before they enter the theatre or other performance space, but we are concerned with all stages of the audience members' journey. What will they experience when they first walk through the doors of the theatre or the school hall? Will they benefit from a low-key introduction to the show in a separate area before they enter the main performance space? We often provide such 'airlocks' between the outside world and the world of the play. How will they be made welcome and intrigued as they enter the main performance space? How will they leave the performance at the end and what will they take away with them? What impressions, ideas, perhaps physical mementoes? Everyone went away from *Baking Time* (2003) with his or her own bun that they had just seen and smelled baking on-stage. For an Oily Cart audience the show should begin long before they encounter a performer, and continue long after they have left the theatre space.

For our work with young people with PMLD or ASD we need to see that the script allows us plenty of movement, from close-up work to long shot and back. Many young people with complex disabilities really benefit from very short range, one-to-one work from the performers, which is why our shows for these audiences have high performer to participant ratios. But we believe that theatre should be a group experience, a social experience. We take care to move from close up moments to sequences in which the rest of the audience and the performers are showcased.

Related to these close-up/long-shot issues are what I sometimes call the 'jazz structure' of our shows. In our work for babies and toddlers, and for young people with complex disabilities, there need to be lengthy periods where the cast improvise, responding to the audience's reactions. So that the whole thing does not become a one-on-one, free-form mush, we factor in precisely scripted and rehearsed passages that bring the whole ensemble back to-gether, performing to the audiences as a whole. These rehearsed passages usually include the opening and the coda, with 'riffs' peppering the rest of the action.

Stage Three: casting

Once we have the script, frequently accompanied by much of the design and some of the music, we come to one of the most significant parts of the Oily process: casting. Oily Cart casts are most often a combination of experienced performers and newcomers.

If you're new to the company then you'll need to be auditioned, most likely by Max Reinhardt, the music director, and myself. We're almost always looking for people who can sing, act and move well, in addition to having some specialist skill, such as puppetry or playing an instrument. We ask anyone auditioning to improvise. Improvising ability is essential because so much of our work re-quires an ability to react fluently to the requirements of the audience.

One of our favourite audition pieces is the 'jam sandwich' test, in which we supply the auditionee with the ingredients to make – perhaps you can guess – a jam sandwich, and ask him or her to show us several versions of the sandwich-making process. The first version, which is to explain the process in its simplest terms so that anyone watching could make a sandwich them-selves, usually causes the most bother. But straightforward explanation is something often called for in our work, as we try to make quite clear to some-one who is very young, or has a severe learning disability, just what is going on.

Stage Four: rehearsals

Anyone who's passed the audition will find themselves part of an ensemble of which at least a half will have had previous experience with the Oily Cart. Although at the start of rehearsal I deliver my tuppence worth about the Oily Cart's methods and the reasons behind them – often bringing in teachers and other experts to supplement my efforts – we usually find the best method of assimilating the Oily Cart approach is to watch the more experienced performers in action with the audience.

Although Max and I also do a good deal of role play as audience members during rehearsals, these uncanny portrayals never seem to impress the new cast members as much as the real thing. It's more useful when we try out parts of the show with the children of Smallwood School, where we are based, or in local Special Needs schools.

Obviously Oily Cart performers need the rehearsals to find their character and to get to grips with the technicalities of their parts, but probably it's even more important that they put themselves in the shoes of their audiences. What will it be like to perform to very young children who still do not use verbal language? How will it be to perform to young people with PMLD who may be unable to hear or see what is going on? How do you best approach young people on the autism spectrum, who may become very anxious when encountering new people or situations? How would you prefer to be approached if you were in a wheelchair? These are a few of the issues that we might approach through role playing, expert advice and discussion during rehearsals

Our rehearsal periods usually last for five weeks, although there are exceptions: for example, we put together *Baby Balloon* with only one week's rehearsal. On the morning of the first day there is a read-through of the script and Max will introduce the music and Claire the set, costume and other design elements. For the next two weeks the mornings of the rehearsal period will be devoted to music rehearsal and the afternoons to what is commonly referred to as 'actin''.

The music rehearsals are concerned with warming up the cast's voices, teaching them the tunes and working out the arrangements. The actin' side of things begins with working out characterisation and how to relate to the audience. We often play theatre games to warm up for this part of the process. Later on we'll concentrate on working out how to actually stage some of the more ambitious stage directions in a script, for example, this section from *Ring a Ding Ding*:

Music of the spheres and very misterioso lighting effects, as puppet captain and puppet Alice first levitate upwards and then begin to fly clockwise over the playboard.

The boat and island are rotated away and the lighting changes as they fly into space itself. Space is evoked by Elayce and Deanne whirling sparklers all round the outside of the audience.

When the sparklers go out, the puppets approach the surface of the moon, with the lunar scenery being whirled into position below them. The captain crash lands.

ALICE: Here we are – on the moon. Look – if you jump you go high in the sky.

Zero gravity play.

Captain bounces on his head, then falls into the centre hole waving his feet in the air.

Many Oily shows, whatever the audience, have substantial moments in which the audience is invited to move around inside the world of the play in what's called a promenade style. This enables the audience to interact with characters and have a direct influence on the way the story develops. The beginnings and the endings of these sections of physical interaction must be very carefully rehearsed if they are to be opportunities for creative play rather than exercises in crowd control.

From the third week onwards it all comes together, and the fifth week will mostly be devoted to technical aspects of the show including lighting, followed by two dress rehearsals and two preview performances with the relevant audience.

So, that's my attempt to describe a 'typical' rehearsal process, but much of our rehearsal time, particularly when we're working on an unusual form of staging, for example in hydro pools or using trapeze or bungee on a high rig, can end up being devoted to technicalities and especially concerns about safety and the comfort of the audience.

But, whether we're floating in the water, flying through the air, or rooted to the stage, the key is to keep the spirit of playfulness and continual experiment in the rehearsal room. When a group of performers gets in the zone the ideas just bubble up. Characters, situations, and lines of dialogue emerge that no amount of laptop pounding could ever produce.

After five weeks the new show is ready to open, but one of the most important parts of the production is missing: the audience.

Stage Five: on the road

An Oily Cart show is usually in an acceptable condition when it opens but it will continue to evolve as it tours. All our productions are so hugely dependent on the reactions of the audiences, and each audience is so different from the one before and the one that follows, that a cast will take some time before they are completely confident in the improvised parts of our shows.

Claire, Max and I are generally present at all performances in the first couple of weeks of a new show, and one or the other of us will continue to monitor a performance each week from then on, giving notes and re-rehearsing as necessary. We also pay a great deal of attention to the comment sheets that our audiences complete and to the reactions of our peers, assessors and the theatre critics – yet another way in which our audiences are, in part, the creators of Oily Cart shows.

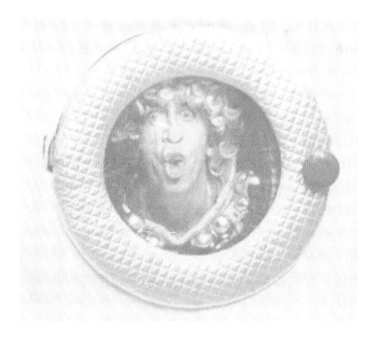

The Art of the Cart:
Designing Oily shows
Claire de Loon

Starting at the beginning

I am fortunate to be working with a brilliant artistic director/writer. Tim and I have been working together on shows since 1971. We share a lot of our enthusiasms such as Chinese opera, Kathakali, traditional puppet forms and so on.

Mostly Tim comes up with the initial themes for the shows. Then we work on developing them together with Max. We are a team who respect each other but know each other well enough to be able to be honest about what we like and don't like. Tim thinks in a very visual way and often helps me with the design. He in turn listens to my suggestions: let's have 60 string babies, one for

Moon puppet from Ring a Ding Ding 2011
Photo: Patrick Barlow

27

each child or let's get the puppets made in South Africa... We both love Max and enjoy working together.

How to gauge what our audience likes

When I go to see one of our shows, I only have eyes for the audience. I am fixated on their reactions to what we are offering them. I want to see them point at things, stroke the textures, squeal when they get sprayed with water, curl up in a blanket or open the box. I want to hear them go 'wow'. I love it when they sit, mesmerised, with eyes like saucers or when they crawl onto the set.

So what do our audiences like?

I think that they like the same things that I do: a strong overall design with a limited palette of colours and materials. The look should reinforce the theme of the show. Many of our shows have been inspired by a material such as paper or string. The fun is to play with all the variations on that material. Other shows have been inspired by the work of a particular artist such as Juan Miro or Lee Bontecou. The design of *Hippity Hop* (2004) relied heavily on the contribution of the graffiti artist Aztek. *Ring a Ding Ding* (2011) has been built around the work of South African wireworker, Mogothi. In other words, the design can be as sophisticated as any work for an adult audience. I have had a lot of fun sharing the visuals that excite me with my audience.

A typical Oily Cart approach is to make the ordinary extraordinary. We want to use situations that are familiar to children, bringing out their potential for magic and wonder.

Personally I love street markets. This aesthetic has inspired *Hippity Hop* and supermarkets were the reference for *George Sells Out* (1996). For *Playhouse* (1999 version), drawings by children at Smallwood School, the South London primary school, the annexe of which has been home to Oily Cart since 1996, inspired the set and the shadow puppets. The children jumping on the bed was a favourite. *Pass the Parcel* (1998) was about the magic of sending a parcel, so the materials included lovely brown paper and string, and the colour scheme was inspired by red postboxes and pale blue Airmail letters. Blue was all about the romance of denim jeans and trains.

When we receive drawings and comments made by children after seeing a show, I am delighted to see how they choose a wide variety of elements as their favourite bits. Which brings me to 'less is more'. Tim and I are constantly saying this when we do training. I ask myself constantly, 'Is this too much? Too many colours? Too much detail?' The answer is usually, 'Yes. It is.' But the realisation of a show is always a series of compromises in order to get a show on, in budget and on time. I try to be true to the principle of simplicity, although my sets have been called 'gloriously louche' and 'fabulously kitsch'. Designing is a process of eliminating the superfluous, but at the same time retaining sufficient detail to appeal to a young audience.

Colour and pattern

When Tim and I met, I was working as an assistant to Philip Prowse at the Citizens Theatre, Glasgow. Philip has been a life-long inspiration and model for me. His sets and costumes were mainly all black. Totally uncompromising, startling and breathtakingly beautiful. Occasionally he did red and gold.

Giles Havergal, who was artistic director of the Citz, recently came to see *Something in the Air* (2009). The concept was that the aerialists – Ockham's Razor – were nesting in a forest canopy. They were simply costumed in scarlet with elaborate, red-tassled hairpieces. The set was an immense frame supporting a dozen green garlanded nest chairs. There were three emerald acrobats' silks that flowed down onto circular emerald carpets. The visual aesthetic was inspired by an Andy Goldsworthy photograph of a single red leaf in an otherwise green tree. Giles approved and I hope that Philip would have too.

Touch, smell, kinaesthetic sense

Doing shows for young people with severe learning disabilities has influenced our mainstream work profoundly. We have developed a house style across the board that addresses as many of the senses as possible.

For Manchester International Festival 2011, we collaborated with Seven Scent, a company who create beautiful perfumes and other not so lovely fragrances. They gave us a smell for *Mole in the Hole* (2010) that conjured up underground leaf mould and damp. For *Gorgeous* (2011), they created signature fragrances for each character and all the resources used such as bubbles, cream and soap suds.

When designing for young people with a visual impairment or for babies whose eyesight has not developed yet, it is important to use bold shapes and colours and to make sure that the actors stand out against a contrasting background.

Preparation, preparation, preparation

It is vital that our audience be pleased to meet the characters in their costumes and to walk into the performance space.

To help with the preparation process, we made our first resource pack for *Playhouse* in 1988. Since then, we have gone to great lengths to create printed materials (such as worksheets and books) that will enhance the experience, particularly for the audience with severe learning disabilities. For young people on the autism spectrum, it is essential. With *Something in the Air*, Nick Weldin used digital technology to create an interactive website, and with *Gorgeous*, we made an interactive social story.

For the very young, we start our performances in the foyer, so front of house is incorporated into the design.

Seating

The seating in mainstream theatre is fairly standard, but in an Oily show it could be anything, from a carpet to a chair that rises two meters above the floor, a bed of bubbles floating in a pool, or a cushion that is part of a matching game.

We have performed for audiences of different sizes, from only two young people and two carers in a water show to a full studio theatre set in a proscenium arch configuration. As a rule, we have an audience of about six young people for a PMLD or ASD show and 30-60 for an early years promenade show. These low audience numbers are now accepted practice by many venues, but it has been a long and hard fought campaign. We feel that it is essential to meaningful interactive theatre.

The challenge of creating an immersive installation that can be toured

'Will it fit in the van?' is a question most designers will recognise. If the set has to create a 360-degree environment in a studio theatre, you have to become adept at finding ways to create a big impact with elements that are as light and easy to fit up as possible.

Our water shows have been an unusual challenge. The size of the pools varies. Some are clinical white expanses, some are covered in Disney mermaids and dolphins, while others are small wooden sauna-style cabins. We needed materials that don't rust, rot or bleach out in chlorine; think plastazote and plastic. We use lighting intended for gardens or divers' torches. To inject bubbles into the water, we use a domestic bath jacuzzi. Boating shops provide pumps to circulate water to our cascades. For safety reasons, we always use 12-volt low-voltage equipment. We have suspended mirror balls from magnets or floated helium filled balloons above the participants.

As well as transforming the pool, we create a 'dry area', a delightful ante-chamber where the participants meet the actors and are gently attuned to the ambiance of the journey. In *Dreams and Secrets* (2000), they entered a huge bed, before entering the sparkling dream itself.

Transforming a studio theatre space is relatively easy. Imaginatively trans-porting a school pool or sports hall to a magical place is more difficult. Even a small amount of stage lighting on stands can add a lot to the impact of the design. The limitations are often down to the school's power supply and smoke alarms.

Occasionally we have created site-specific installations. I really enjoyed work-ing on a grand scale with *Under Your Hat* (2001) on the dance floor of the Royal Festival Hall.

Is it washable?
Doing interactive work means that everything has to look good up close while being able to withstand being grabbed, sucked and more.

Lighting
We have been fortunate to have had some superb lighting designers who have enhanced the designs exponentially: people like Natasha Chivers, Chris Davey, Anna Watson and Jack Knowles.

Puppets
Oily Cart has used puppets in nearly all its shows for the very young. We prefer not to have adults playing a baby or a small child but a puppet can do the job very well.

Red Lorry, Yellow Lorry (1990) featured actors dressed as lorries. The miniature lorries hung from their shoulders on braces. The drivers were small glove puppets. The actors travelled around the audience, while the children reached up to touch the vehicles because they liked them so much.

We rarely use puppets in our shows for young people with profound and multiple learning disabilities. They prefer people, up close and relating to their every reaction.

However, in *Drum* (2010), in the version for junior aged children on the autism spectrum, we introduced a child-sized puppet. He had large velvety arms that were heavily weighted and could wrap around a child. He proved a useful intermediary between the performers and the audience.

Boxes and little twinkly lights

The moon and the stars are recurring themes in Oily shows. We love star cloths and mirror balls. You need a blackout for these to be effective so we save them for the end of the show when the children are confident enough to be comfortable in the dark.

Little boxes or houses preferably with lights inside, are another leitmotif. For *Big Splash* (1999), Michael Charlton made us a set of little sensory boxes with a fountain, a rotary dryer and a revolving hot sun inside.

Nests also appear in a number of shows, the most spectacular being *Conference of the Birds* (2004). Rachel James made a pair of inflatable wings that wrapped around the entire audience. Lit from within, they were glorious.

Is there a difference between designing for neurotypical early years children, and children and young people with severe learning disabilities?

Not really. I think that all these audiences respond to a beautiful looking show. It has to be beautiful. Nothing else will do.

Having fun

In the course of the past 30 years, I have had to learn a lot of fun things. For *Baby Balloon* (2006) I learned how to make balloon hats from artist Addi Somekh. The set for *Big Balloon* (2006) was made entirely of balloons. I have also learned a lot about baking bread, knotting rope, Turkish baths and trampolining.

Looking back over the company's reviews, fun is a word that often appears. We too have had fun making our lovely audiences happy.

Working with great people

Working with Tim and Max has been the best thing of all. I have also had the privilege of working with many wonderful designers, artists and makers. I have already mentioned some. Here are a few more old friends that I would like to thank: Simon Auton, Patrick Baldwin, Sue Dacre, Jens Demant Cole, Mary Edwards, Pat Farmer, Karen Grosch, Jamie Linwood, Holly Murray, Maija Nygren, Nik Ramage, Jonny Stockbridge, Nick Weldin and Dave Whetton.

CartBeat – Making Music for Oily Cart
Max Reinhardt

Oily Cart have travelled a long road – possibly constructing it en route – in the direction of a form of theatre in which all its discrete art forms are becoming ever more closely integrated. At the start of our creative relationship, I knew little about how music and theatre shape each other or the creative opportunities of this fissile mix.

Like many others of the post World War II generation in the UK, my limited experience of music theatre as a child was through musicals, mostly imported from the US, pantomime, and, when I was lucky, variety. We were swimming in vast oceans of music for TV and film, of course. However, by the time I was a teenage wannabe musician in 60s London, the only musical game in town that interested me was to become a live electric and acoustic musician, playing in bands or solo, fed by a varied diet of pop, rock, blues, jazz, folk and

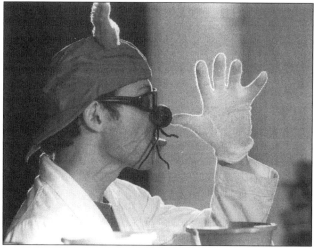

Max as the Cat in Seaside 1985

33

experimental music. But that kind of musical career didn't quite happen for me in the way I originally imagined. By the mid-seventies I was based at Battersea Arts Centre, writing and performing songs with children, in schools, playgroups and family workshops.

Increasingly inspired by the fringe and street theatre companies all around me, I began composing and arranging songs for the productions of children's theatre company Theatre Kit, and also working with Tim (Webb) and Claire (de Loon) on various projects, one of which became our Exploding Punch and Judy Show.

So when the Oily Cart started, what did I bring to the party, musically speaking? Basic guitar, piano and singing skills, an aptitude for making up catchy tunes, often on the spot, sometimes with hordes of children, and much experience born of hours of singing and making music with primary school and pre-school children. My approach arose totally out of my experience of creating music with bands, rather than any kind of formal education in musical direction. It still does. I come in with ideas based around the script and/or discussions with Tim and Claire, be they melodies, starting points for improvisation, chants, lyrics, rhythms, found sounds or chord sequences; then we realise them in rehearsal with the performers, both musicians and non-musicians. As it has turned out, this approach has very much coincided with Tim's approach to theatre.

The 30 years of continuous evolution in our work is based on a continuum of ideas, approaches and shared enthusiasms that have flourished between us. Our work has always explored stories, performances, visions and sounds that, in the first place, excite and delight us, and also present us with new challenges – not least how to communicate that excitement and share our delight with our audiences. Tim's passions have always extended way beyond script, plot and character to include visual and musical elements. So the frenzied priorities of the rehearsal process have always more than adequately included and integrated those areas: it is a distinctive Oily Cart *modus operandi*.

Perhaps even more essentially for our music, Tim and I discovered from our earliest days a shared hinterland of obsessive diverse and arcane musical interests. While we drove around London in late 1981, performing in different schools and nurseries twice a day, shows featuring participative songs played on a beaten up twelve-string guitar and Casio VL Tone VL-1 mini keyboard, the music chat in the Renault 12 Estate was all about Miles Davis, John Coltrane, Derek Bailey, Frank Zappa and Captain Beefheart, etc. Experimentation had to be the musical path to which we aspired.

At first, the curve was shallow and reflected in our use of what were then newer 'pop' musical styles like disco (*Bus Stop*, 1982), rap (*Down The Plughole*, 1984), nu skool r 'n' b (*Slipped Disco*, 1986) and our adoption of ever fresher and more ingenious products from the new burgeoning digital keyboard industry. The younger members of our families were urging us on enthusiastically.

At the same time roots music was always an important part of our musical palette, and I added banjo, ukelele and accordion to my basic instrumental skills repertoire. Increasingly, the music supported the theatre stylistically: gothic organ for *Bats in their Belfry* (1982), pastiche sea shanties for *Parrots of Penzance* (1984), a 'Ukrainian' accordion folk ballad for the Caterpillar in Picnic (1985), songs written using Egyptian (Arabic) scales for *Curse of the Mummy's Sphinx* (1987).

Notably, for *Soapsuds* (1985), Tim suggested we embark on an Oily version of sound art. With the help of sound sculptor and artist Max Eastley, we became sensitised to the 'found' sounds around us, and created a score based on acapella singing and the percussive qualities of the set. Sound art, acapella singing and percussion have since become a regular part of our sound palette, most recently in the music made from paper of *If All the World Were Paper* (2005 and 2007) and the junk pitched percussion and sea and fog soundscapes of *Ring A Ding Ding* (2011).

Box of Socks (1988), our first show in schools for young people with severe learning difficulties (SLD), was a watershed show for us right across the board. In the musical realm, it introduced not just live improvisation with a toy sampler (Casio SK-1), one-on-one with each member of the audience, but also another intriguing development. For the previous five years, outside my life with Oily Cart, I had become, first of all, a mobile DJ and then a tropical music club DJ. Tim suggested that I bring that experience, and my double turntables, into the show. So, the aliens from Planet Sox who visited the school ended the day and the show with an exquisite inter-planetary disco that somehow managed to mix the Afrobeat of Fela Anikulapo Kuti with early Kylie Minogue anthems! In the years ahead, we would often utilise the musical knowledge, skills and contacts of my musical work outside Oily Cart to enhance the shows, often at Tim's suggestion.

None of the above, by the way, denies the music hall influence that still can be traced in our use of song for routines; eg 'When I Look In My Mirror' (*Up On The Roof*, 1986), 'Going to the Fair' (*EuroBroadbent*, 1993) or 'How Do You Hold a Baby?' (How Long is a Piece of String, 2008).

As the eighties ended and Tim and I began to step back from continuous frontline performing into our roles as artistic and musical directors, we started to work with actor/musicians, which potentially meant more complex arrangements, with more voices and more instruments. Thanks to ground-breaking computer software that became available, even musicians who didn't play by ear but required music scores could join us. The core ensemble that we fostered through the nineties notably included the instrumental and vocal talents of Geoff 'Pex' Bowyer, Sue Eves, Sjaak van der Bent , Caroline Hier and Carol Walton. With them our musical excursions became more flexible and I could write to their musical strengths.

Acapella singing was revisited with the singing nurses of *Will It Hurt?* (1990) and the singing postpersons of *Pass the Parcel* (1998). Sound art resurfaced notably in *Funky Philharmonic* (1991), with homemade instruments from re-cycled materials made by Echo City and Will Embliss, and mass scratch orchestras formed by the students in each school we visited. Rap resurfaced in Play House (1999), this time totally live with a brass band. Various world music flavours tipped over, absorbed from my club DJ experiences; salsa (Red Lorry Yellow Lorry, 1990; *A Bit Missing*, 1993; and *Tickled Pink*, 1996), South African township jive (*Pleasure Dome*, 1989; and *Greenfingers*, 1992), country and cajun for the cowboy carpenter in *Fishing for Pigs* (1993); the hens in *A Peck of Pickled Pepper* (1994); and the useless handyman with his musical saw in *Off the Wall* (1991).

The two-day shows for young people with SLD demanded a lot of music for a variety of theatrical purposes. The idea of a marching band, which performed at the end of the day to play the students onto their homebound buses, emerged in *Colour Me Colour You* (1990). We call them 'bus busks' and they continue to bring theatre and music live and thumping right into the heart of the everyday reality of our audience.

The playlets that made up each show often used specific complementary design and styles of music to pack their punch; such as the trance-like set and music for the sections of *After a Fashion* (1995), which were performed with students with profound and multiple learning disabilities (PMLD). In those sessions we personalised the song for each student, singing about what they were doing, which led to our concept of the 'name song'; a technique that re-mains a constant feature in our shows for these audiences. The name of each student is sung by the ensemble, hopefully beautifully, and with the addition of mirror or video. For a little while, the whole show is just about that student.

We had undoubtedly been closing in on the target for a while but, for me, it was in *George Sells Out* (1996), the final two-day show we created for audiences with SLD, that we arrived at a production in which every element – plots, characters, design and music – worked in a wholly integrated way to create the world of George's Supermarket. Call it genre immersion, total theatre or what you will, but Tim's supermarket concept brought out the best in all of us. He asked for muzak – the canned, middle-of-the-road soundtrack that used to dominate shopping malls and hypermarkets. The songs, backing tracks and live blowing definitely took you right into the territory and, perversely, we all loved it!

Our game had been well and truly upped, and that total theatre concept remains our grail, whether writ gloriously large (*Something in the Air*, 2009) or as a beautiful miniature (*Drum*, 2010). It certainly bloomed in *Roly Poly Pudding* (1996), which took its under-fives audience into a world filled with human-powered mechanical sculptures and simple geometry, where even the music was cranked out of a fairground organ, and music for triangles was in 3/4, music for squares in 4/4 and music for circles in everlasting loops.

The decade and the century ended with our series of water shows for PMLD audiences that set a series of new musical challenges. We rejoiced in the sound of the water itself, the idea of water drumming and the sonic ambience of the pools, but the musical elements required evolution and that immersive Oily Cart vision.

Since the scratch orchestras of *Funky Philharmonic* we had become interested in finding ways and means of facilitating musical participation from young people with limited voluntary movement. In *Over The Moon* (1997) we conceived of a pentatonic scratch chime bar orchestra, utilising the wobbly 'sound buoys' of our now renowned musical instrument inventor Jamie Linwood, who has a PhD in pitched percussion, and who I found via the musical instrument making department at East London University. But how would that work in the water? With floating sound buoys, of course – they sounded their metallic and wooden 'chimes' when they were bobbed by water or by our audience.

Crucially, how would we produce live pitched music in the watery atmosphere? *Dreams and Secrets* (2002) began its life with a vision vouchsafed to Claire and Tim in a hammam (bath house) in Istanbul, where they were enchanted to find a woman singing beautifully in the water. Inspired by that notion we created acapella pieces that were accompanied by the sound of water and near eastern(ish), jazz(ish) pieces in which vocal harmony, water and sax or clarinet were delicately blended.

The following year with *Waving* (2003), Tim and Claire's concept of a West African watery idyll brought me to the balafons, the marimba-like instruments of countries like Mali and Senegal. It was amazingly liberating to write the music on instruments I'd never played before, inspired by some of the melodies I'd spent the last decade listening to. Although at that stage I didn't know of any African musicians who were available, I knew that if I could play the music a little, a sensitive percussionist/singer could certainly play it better, and Suzanne Worrica fulfilled and exceeded my expectations. Our most recent water-based show, *Pool Piece* (2008), was similarly based around tuned percussion, which is traditionally played near water, but this time it was the regal splendour of the sounds of gamelan instruments from Bali, loaned to us courtesy of Jamie Linwood.

In the early noughties we embarked on shows for babies with a looser, changing ensemble that included vocals and playing from Patrick Lynch, Nicole Worrica and Ruth Calkin. The music for the baby audience for *Jumpin' Beans* (2002) [there were two versions of the show, one for children aged three to six, the other for babies] focused on simplicity of melody. It had to be catchy enough for parents and minders to coo along with to their babies. In contrast, the music for the two visits to the Boing Club (*Boing!*, 2002; and *Moving Pictures*, 2003), which Tim located in 50s Beirut for the purposes of sonic, musical and visual inspiration, was more complex. The backing tracks were created from samples of found sound (some from libraries, some recorded when I was on tour in Tunis) – bubbled under samples of ouds , kanuns and derboukas – which blended into my original, maghrebi-inspired compositions. In performance they were improvised over, vocally and instrumentally, by the cast as our PMLD audience took magic carpet rides on the trampoline.

In 2004, *Conference of the Birds* and *Hippity Hop* continued this use of samples, backing tracks, real sound recordings and live singing and playing. With Birds, it adopted a minimalist, ceremonial form, complementing the near-sacred quality of the design and the formality and security of ritual that Tim breathed into our incarnation of the Palace of the Birds specifically for our audience of young people with complex disabilities and/or autistic spectrum disorders (ASD). *Hippity Hop* took hip hop and r 'n' b-inspired melodies and beats to its pre-school and baby audiences; its grittier, urban, funky musical approach contrasted with the clean, gentle simplicity of *Jumpin'*

Beans. The backing tracks blended sounds from the streets of South London with hip hop beats and keyboards, topped off by scratching from Steve '$6Million Turntablist' Austin, and backing vocals from the Mint Juleps. The raps written by Bries and Jonzi D were performed by a cast that included a rapper (Paul Bonnelamme, aka The Southside Assassin) and Mark Foster, a veteran performer in Oily cart shows who has severe learning difficulties, un-bounded optimism and can-do spirit, and, fortunately for the music, a stun-ningly low bass singing voice.

From the point of view of musicians, *Hippity Hop* very much exemplified a new phase in making music for Oily Cart. Over the past decade, we've mostly built the music around specialist full-time musicians rather than actor/musicians. That's partly a response to the sound of the music that we think the shows require, and partly a desire for new musical collaborations. It's cer-tainly true that we've become better placed on the margins of the merry-go-round of the music biz to attract sometimes even quite well-known musi-cians and vocalists onto backing tracks and into shows, including: jazzers like Jason Yarde and Byron Wallen; folk musicians like Eliza Carthy, Saul Rose and Martin Green; cabaret/theatre musicians like Kathy Toy; classical musicians like Sophie Solomon and Zoë Martlew; and a whole host of amazing percus-sionists including Salah Dawson Miller, Hami Lee, Karim Delali and Usifu Jalloh.

Notably, I was joined for the premiere run of *Baby Balloon* (2006) in Brussels by Ernst Reijsiger, the astonishing Dutch jazz/contemporary classical cellist, and we created an improvised score that brought together all manner of styles of cello playing, from spinning cello to township jazz, with electronica, harmonica, toys and balloon sounds. Creating music for a dance show for babies proved a very liberating musical experience for us, and underscored an extraordinary abstract visual, tactile and emotional experience in which babies and parents alike became totally absorbed.

The year 2006 was also the one that Griff Fender, formerly a singer in seventies chart band Darts, joined our casts. His vocal abilities and general musicality have enhanced our shows ever since. That would include the songs for *Blue*, which emerged from my immersion in delta blues and old-time music, sometimes accompanied by harmonica virtuoso Errol Linton, but always underpinned by the guitar work of Chad Hague or Ben Smith.

Early discussions between Tim, Claire and me meant that only music pro-duced by string instruments could feature in *How Long is a Piece of String* (2008), so I wrote the music with Nik Ammar, guitarist with nu-klezmer band

Oi Va Voi. Nik accompanied the show live with instruments ranging from double bass to charango and the adept use of a pedal, with melodies that ranged from Latin American to Congolese via rocking blues, as the cast and audience set out on their voyage to bring the 'babies' home.

In early rehearsals for *Something in the Air* (2009), our aerial collaboration with Ockham's Razor, I tried all manner of 'airy' sound samples. Then, probably because my radio work (I'm a regular presenter on the voyage into uncharted waters that is BBC Radio Three's *Late Junction*) was beginning to extend my musical education, I got inspiration from the proms, where I was transfixed by the solo clarinet movement of Messaien's *Quartet for the End of Time*, which happens to be entitled The Abyss of Birds. So clarinet definitely became 'the way', and all roads then led fortuitously to Arun Ghosh, ace clarinettist and multi-instrumentalist.

The music was partly composed and partly improvised between us and, in the event, in order to underscore the moods and movements of the aerialists, extended beyond the dominant clarinet to percussion, harmoniums, drones and much else. The lyricism of the music certainly enhanced the majesty of the show, the aerial mastery of the Ockhams, the ingenuity of the concept and the magic of its audience responding and rejoicing in mid-air.

Consequently, Arun was also lead or sole live musician for the two early years shows that followed: on clarinet, keyboard and kitchen percussion for *Christmas Baking Time* (2009), and on bass clarinet for the underground sound of *Mole in the Hole* (2010).

The trio of *Drum* (2010/11) shows and our current show *Ring a Ding Ding* (2011) bring the musical saga of the Cart up to date. They rely on the instrument-making prowess of Jamie Linwood, aforementioned genius inventor and maker of percussion instruments. It seemed as if Tim had commissioned Jamie to build a giant drum out of the hide of a Thai water buffalo even before he had conceived of a show that would return us to our roots and be small enough to tour nurseries as well as play studio theatres. Once the astonishingly mighty hand drum had arrived, we made the show using the techniques of our earliest creations, and made it all up with the cast on the floor. The melodies, rhythms and pairing of voices and percussion nod towards the Sierra Leonean origins of both the percussionists who worked on the show, Usifu Jalloh and George Panda, and all elements of the show certainly issue forth from the drums.

Jamie's instrument-making virtuosity extended to creating *Ring a Ding Ding*'s collection of tuned scaffolding pipes, chunks of car chassis and aluminium offcuts, which somehow cross the sound of gamelan pots with steel pan. Tim and Claire's idea of mounting the whole splendid pile of scrap onto our ancient ice cream tricycle meant that the music, recycled instruments and dream percussionist, George Panda, could go round and round along with the story, the characters, the set, the costumes and the audience.

So, for me, that's every beat of the Cart in a nutshell: making music that is theatre and, indeed, theatre that is music.

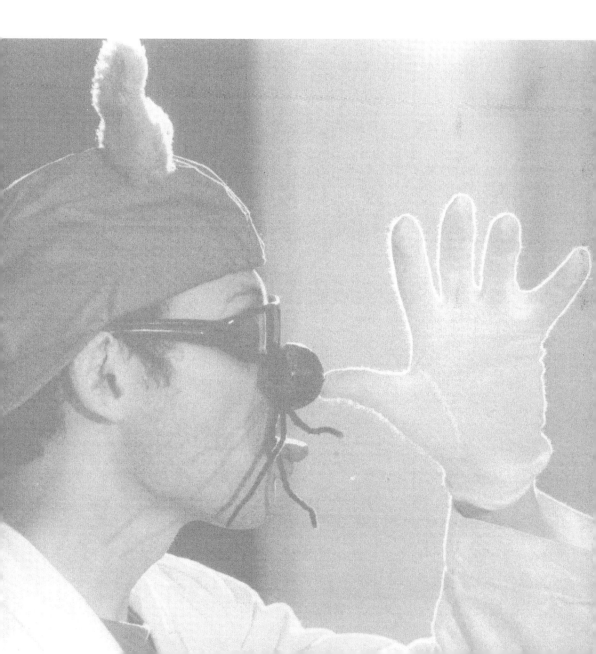

Three Shows:
Blue, Baby Balloon and
Ring a Ding Ding

The following section focuses upon three shows, *Blue, Baby Balloon* and *Ring a Ding Ding*, which reflect the breadth of Oily Cart's work. The shows were designed for three distinct audiences, namely: 1) children and young adults with profound and multiple learning disabilities; 2) babies and toddlers; and 3) children aged two to five years old. In each case, the show is considered from the points of view of the artists themselves, audience members and critics. The inclusion of the complete script of *Blue* offers a wonderful glimpse of how Tim Webb (as writer and director) begins the Oily Cart process at a textual level.

Making *Blue*

The blues are played from Memphis to Mali. An intimate show for young people with complex disabilities and/or an autistic spectrum disorder, involving original live music, innovative lighting, and interactive video projection, *Blue* took place within a specially constructed installation. The audience were invited to enter this 'wonderland', which evoked the sights, sounds and smells of the Deep South, and spend some time with Belle, Lightnin', Champion, Ace, Skip and Big Jack, as they awaited the arrival of their train.

Blue toured Special Needs schools in the UK in summer 2006 and from May to October 2007, including a three-week residency at the Unicorn Theatre, London.

Mark Brown talked about the making of the show with writer and director Tim Webb, designer Claire de Loon and musical director Max Reinhardt.

Blue 2007

Tim Webb
Writing and directing *Blue*

Blue was conceived as a piece for people with profound and multiple learning disabilities, at the same time as being a show for people with an autistic spectrum disorder. We'd already done *Conference of the Birds* the year before (2004-05), and we were very conscious with that piece that we wanted to make a show that would not cause sensory overload for audience members, particularly people on the autistic spectrum. We wanted to put things in a very clear structure, so that people who are having issues with processing information would have time to be absolutely sure where they were in the show and what was happening to them.

What you see in *Blue* is an attempt to create a minimal piece. The set looks clean, it's basically off-white. The particular ways in which things happen is absolutely key: the action stops; things go quiet; then you hear a sound cue; then you see a video projection of what's coming up next; then you actually get the real activity, involving the actors using props and interacting with the audience.

That is conceived of as good practice in autism spectrum disorder (ASD) terms; that's what you'd be enjoined to do by teachers who work with ASD students. You'd be asked to be careful to give them time to absorb things intellectually and emotionally.

Blue came out of our experience of doing *Conference of the Birds*, but I think we did it better with *Blue*. It was really effective and engaged the audience more.

The genesis of blue as a theme came out of my interest in creating an environment that was starkly minimal and into which we'd introduce a sound, or a colour, or a texture, but only one thing at a time. Then you would withdraw that element, and go onto the next thing.

I was thinking of the colour blue you get if you have a television that's not tuned to a channel – TV blue. I was discussing that concept with Claire and we thought, in terms of music, '*Blue*? It's got to be the blues, hasn't it?' And we both really like the blues. We were thinking of the blues as the origins of rock 'n' roll and, more particularly, country blues of the 1930s, Robert Johnson and Blind Willie McTell, Blind Willie Johnson and Blind Willie this, that and the other, you know? It was that kind of guitar blues we were thinking of, and the theme developed from that. We went from the colour TV blue to the blues.

This idea of keeping everything in a show related in some way to the original theme always seems to be very productive with Oily Cart shows. If you say, 'It's all going to be about a piece of string,' (*How Long is a Piece of String*, 2008), and you make everything about string or rope – in sound, in texture, in colour, in action – it's productive. It's like writing a song or a poem, the feeling evoked by the idea takes you into uncharted territory. You end up going to places you wouldn't go if you hadn't given yourself that sort of context. If you write a sonnet, you're going to surprise yourself with the language you come up with, because it's generated in part by the form. It's similar with Oily Cart: in giving ourselves these themes, we encourage our minds to go into interesting areas. It's a nice paradox; it is the structure that liberates you.

We were also influenced by the French visual and performance artist Yves Klein, who actually has a blue (International Klein *Blue*) named after him. Add to that, my favourite album of all time is Miles Davis's *Kind of Blue*. Whatever the musical influences of jazz on the work of Oily Cart – and there are plenty, you can hear them in Max Reinhardt's music – the freedom of jazz also has a big influence on the dramatic structure of our work.

I always loved the way Duke Ellington and Charles Mingus worked. I remember seeing Ellington and his band on the telly way back in the 50s, it'll have been *Sunday Night at the London Palladium*. The band was this amazing collection of individuals with a great variety of playing styles, but Ellington held it all together. He provided a context in which these wonderful human beings could flourish. That's my ideal of how a band, or a theatre company for that matter, should work.

When it comes to casting, it's great when you find a really original performer and you can make a space for them to flourish within the dramatic structure. Take, for example, Griff Fender (long-time Oily Cart performer and founder member of seventies doo-wop revival band Darts). What you have to do is find a Griff-shaped space to let him rip in.

In a similar vein, we worked with Geoff Bowyer (another ex-rock and roller veteran of the 60s band The Purple Gang). Geoff, better known as Pex, was and remains brilliantly funny. He was the undisputed star of our shows for children with special educational needs, in which he frequently played a character called George Broadbent. George was a supreme example of an adult, an authority figure, who would be losing it all the time. To this day staff in Special Needs schools ask after George.

We've often been told that kids with learning disabilities are forever being told what to do, how to behave and where to go. All kids find it amusing when adults lose control, but the kids in Special Needs schools find it really amusing.

In terms of the diversity of our casts the great thing about *Blue* was that, being set in the United States in the early-twentieth century, we're talking about a society with a big immigrant population. We had a Dutchman in the cast and a Portuguese guy from Mozambique and because there would have been such people in the States at that time, we could let them be very richly themselves.

Also, the characters had one piece of luggage, which contained their most treasured possession. In the preparatory material for the show, we asked audience members to bring their piece of luggage, with their most treasured possession. So it turned out to be a very rewarding theme for us.

Claire de Loon
Designing *Blue*

Funnily enough, from a design point of view, the colour blue didn't come into it all that much. My brief was to try to create a touring set that would evoke the setting of the play. So I was trying to evoke an outdoor space that was something like a train station, and something like a porch in the Deep South of the United States.

I also tried to get a flavour of the drive-in movie. A quarter of the space was the projection screen, and we projected an image that introduced each scene. At the very end, when the train came, it was projected onto the screen, with stage smoke, so it seemed to be coming into the space. It was a very dramatic effect, because this train was what all the kids and the characters had been waiting for, and they all jumped up and started running around with excitement because the train had come.

It was the first time we'd used such a large projection screen, and we also used a wide-angle lens video projector. The idea came from the American associations of the piece.

It's typical of our work that there is this interplay between theme and function, that everything we do in terms of design and music, for example, is always trying to go in the same direction as the theme of the show. Everything has to reinforce the other elements of the piece.

We aim to create a space that is welcoming and comfortable, both emotionally comfortable and physically comfortable for the needs of the audience. Some of our audience have issues regarding physical support because they are wheelchair users, and we have to consider how they can best be positioned to enjoy the show.

We have to consider how they can see the show. For example, if a person can't hold their head up, they need to be supported so that they're able to look in the right direction. It's something you take for granted when you're dealing with able-bodied people.

The swinging leaf chairs we use in some of our shows are very good when it comes to supporting people with disabilities. They're very comfortable, they're supportive and you can move them around so that the young person is facing in the appropriate direction. They're also good in a kinaesthetic sense, because you can swing them and bounce them.

In *Blue* we had a lot of rocking chairs and garden swing seats (as well as a couple of leaf chairs), which fitted well with the idea of the veranda, but it also addressed the kinaesthetic question. Kids who are very fidgety could get rid of a lot of that energy through rocking, and still be able to focus on what was happening in the show. That was a good example of the way I try to use design to cater to both the thematic and functional needs of the show.

Just getting over the threshold into the performance space can be a real challenge for some of our audience. In *Blue* there was a very wide opening and you could actually watch the show from outside, and the young people could shuffle in gradually as they became less afraid. This only applies to a small minority of the audience but you have to cater for them too. They wouldn't be able to participate at all if you didn't take these things into account.

We did two other things for those young people. The first sight you got of the set was seeing what was inside from the outside; it was just the shadows of the actors inside the installation. That was a gradual introduction to what was inside, to demystify it and take the element of surprise out of it. So the young people got an introduction to what was coming next.

There were also little windows in the set that audience members could look through. So if you weren't even comfortable with being at the large opening, you could just peer in through one of the little windows. Consequently, we had very little problem with people who couldn't participate at all. Everybody was able to see, including observers such as parents, who wanted to see the show without being seen by the young people in the audience and without intruding on their 360-degree experience.

In terms of costumes, they were American work wear, on the whole. A lot of denim, so the colour blue came in there. Everything looked very washed out, very used and very comfortable. The textures were mainly denim but we also had some nice towels. The shakers were little bandanas with the shakers inside. We had lots of old suitcases and trunks – there was a wooden trunk with a cast iron pump inside of it, which pumped real water. We also used folded paper fans.

At the end, we gave everybody a printed fan, like the ones they use in churches in the Deep South, and that had an image of a train on it. It was a visual and sensory souvenir of the show.

Because of the way we create Oily Cart shows, I'm more involved with connecting design to, for instance, props or the use of music or the requirements of the audience than most theatre designers. Also, I do most of the preparation and resources materials for schools. Tim, Max and I call ourselves 'the creative core' – we all have backgrounds in education, but I take on the editing and putting together of all the teaching material.

Max Reinhardt
Making music for *Blue*

There is obviously a very musical starting point for *Blue*, namely the blues from the Mississippi Delta. Musically, it spills over from the blues into what's called old time music, I guess. But in essence we're looking at the music of poor blacks and poor whites from the Delta, particularly blacks. Tim, Claire and I have a shared enthusiasm for the blues from way back. So there was something to inspire all of us when it came to making the piece.

The blues are the DNA of popular music. The structure of popular music everywhere is heavily influenced by the blues and, interestingly, that feeds back into Africa, which is where the blues originated. You can hear the roots of the blues in a lot of Malian and Senegalese riffs. It goes right across West Africa, really.

One of the things about Oily Cart is that we do work with the things that inspire and excite us. Then we have to find a way of communicating that and sharing that interest and curiosity with the different audiences we have. Some of those audiences are very different from us.

At the outset of the project we were talking about how blues songs are often about lost love, or somebody walking off with your woman or your man, or venereal disease or alcoholism. We asked ourselves, 'How age appropriate is this, and how can we make it work for kids with complex learning disabilities?' Slowly, when we'd sorted out all the things the show couldn't be about, we realised of course that at the core of the blues there is this thing about travelling and trains.

I did the lyrics for *Blue*. I don't always do the lyrics; sometimes Tim does them, sometimes we do them together, and other times I do them. Often they'll get changed on the rehearsal floor anyway. In this case, I could go away and write the songs because I knew at the start that they were all about travelling.

I remember reading Bob Dylan's book *Chronicles: Volume 1* around the time that we made the show. I hadn't realised before reading the book that for the first two or three years that he was in New York he mostly didn't write songs – he played other people's songs, he researched songs. He immersed himself in what we now call Americana. Then he created his own work. What I definitely did, in making the music for *Blue*, was immerse myself more thoroughly in the blues than I ever had before.

Another thing Tim, Claire and I did, before we started creating the show proper in our different departments was to spend a week in Bradford with a theatre company called Mind the Gap, who all have disabilities. Throughout the week we worked with them making a scratch show for kids with severe learning difficulties, and it finished off with two performances. It was a great experience, and a very rare thing.

This was very close to the time we were doing *Blue* and we said to each other that we would try '*Blue* ideas' out in the process of the project in Bradford. I improvised a couple of songs with a slide guitar, for instance. So before we started rehearsing *Blue*, we knew we were all on the same page because of the work we'd been doing with Mind the Gap.

One of the questions I'd been asking myself was, 'What will kids with severe learning difficulties or autistic spectrum disorder think of a slide guitar?' That's the kind of question we have to consider with every show: 'Will anyone be interested in this? Is anyone going to freak out because of this? Is anyone going to feel what I feel from this?' We had a chance to find out all kinds of things, in all departments of the show, during that week in Bradford.

So my approach to the music for *Blue* came from both an immersion in the blues and an immersion in the world of kids with complex learning diffi-culties. We were able to have a very free, workshop approach to this because we were working with actors, as well as audiences who had some of those difficulties.

The music in *Blue* seems to be amongst the most popular of any of the shows we've done. Certainly that was borne out in terms of the feedback we got from teachers and others. At one of the in-service sessions in schools, a teacher said that what he liked about the show was the way it made everybody feel part of a sort of blues community, and plugged us into a culture we all under-stood... and I think you could feel that.

It's very much the case that the songs are part of the action, and the action is part of the songs. For example, one of the songs is about water. While that's being sung, one of the characters produces a water pump from inside his trunk, and there's a whole bubble and splashing water thing going on. It meant that you didn't know how long the piece of music was going to be – it might have to be ten bars shorter or 30 bars longer, depending on how much the kids got into what was happening.

A final *Blue* story that brings trains and music together: we were a few months away from starting rehearsals for the second tour of *Blue* and the original guitarist on the show had left to become a surveyor. So one day I happened to be at Liverpool Street station in London. I wasn't thinking specifically about the show, but the fact that we needed a blues guitarist was obviously at the back of my mind. Suddenly I heard someone finger picking a blues rag thing, and I thought, 'Blimey, that's it!' I watched him for a while and I couldn't decide whether he was busking for a fix (these are the streets of London, after all) or this was his daily job, and he made enough money and had a mortgage and all that. I followed my hunch, we auditioned him (Ben Smith), and he was just perfect. In fact, it all fitted in for him, too, because he was about to become a dad and wanted something that was a bit more regular than busking, but not too regular. He really was an acoustic blues man, as much as a white boy busking in London can be.

Audience feedback for *Blue* (2007)

The project was brilliant. The kids got loads out of it and were always excited to see Boom Boom and the rest of the Oily Cart team. It reached the kids on different levels.

A huge sensory/communication tool, very beneficial to both pupils and staff.

Refreshingly different, creative and reflective. The project has provided inspiration for further creative activities and use of a 'problem' space.

The project was a brilliant experience for children and staff. The interaction from the children was fabulous to see. The Oily Cart people are very special, just like our children are to us. They are the best.

A truly life-changing experience – never to be forgotten. The empathy of the theatre group was wonderful. The activities were perfectly in tune with the needs of the students. The ever-changing setting in the quad was exciting... their presence has had a really positive effect on staff and students. It's the best thing I have ever seen in a school in 24 years. Brilliant!

Feedback from schools

There can be no clearer example of the transforming power of the arts than the extraordinary work that the Oily Cart theatre company did with Special Needs schools as part of the Manchester International Festival.

James Purnell,
then Secretary of State for Culture, Media and Sport, July 2007

Review

The following review of *Blue*, by Lyn Gardner, appeared in the *Guardian* on July 5, 2006.

Oily Cart is one of the great British theatre companies of the last 25 years. Yet plenty of theatregoers, even the most avid, will not have heard of it. The reason is simple: Oily Cart works entirely with children, many with complex disabilities, and often behind closed doors in Special Needs schools.

This has made the company focus more specifically on its audience and environment: you can't make text and narrative-heavy theatre for an audience who have limited language skills, and a school hall is often an entirely unpromising theatrical space. As a result Oily Cart has developed a theatrical style that is multisensory. It has also become exceptionally skilled at creating environments within environments, placing the company at the forefront of theatrical experimentation in this country.

Blue, currently at the Unicorn Theatre for Children, is inspired by the sounds and images of blues music. It is not one of the company's most radical pieces, but it gives a real taste of its ability to communicate directly with its audience – young people with severe disabilities and their carers.

The Unicorn's Clore Studio has been transformed into a tented space which, with its swing seats and rocking chairs, has the feel of a station porch somewhere in the Deep South. Here as we wait for the train, musicians sing and play while the passengers reveal the contents of their luggage: water to splash, stars to handle, a fan to create a cool breeze, a video camera to capture the image of a laughing child being serenaded. What's interesting about the work is the way it breaks down all the traditional barriers between performer and audience and the rules that cast the actors as active and the audience as passive. The show opens with the children offering up the contents of their own 'blues boxes' of precious memories and objects.

This is not a theatrical experience that you watch, but one that you all share. Other contemporary theatre-makers should take note.

The Script of *Blue*
By Tim Webb

Cast:

CHAMPION, with the Suitcase of Stars.. Mark Foster

BLUE BELLE, with the Parcel of Fans..Carys Williams

BIG JACK, with the Washday Blues Bag...................................Sjaak Van Der Bent

ACE, with the Guitar Case.. Chad Hague

LIGHTNIN', with the Trunk-full of Memories...............................Edgar Oliveira

SKIP, Company Stage Manager...Griff Fender

First Scene

On the way to the installation:

As the visitors and their companions approach the installation they can hear the sounds of the warning bells on a US-style railroad crossing, a train whistle and other sounds of a departing train. Wisps of steam swirl across the floor.

They see the silhouettes of the travellers on the walls of the installation: BELLE is rocking in her chair and talking to CHAMPION.

If there are to be a number of wheelchair users involved in a particular session, and hoisting is likely, then most of the cast should stay outside the porch installation and help with getting the visitors from the wheelchairs and into their seats as and when required. Only ACE need stay on the porch and keep the music going while the visitors are settled in.

On the other hand, if most of our visitors are mobile and especially if a majority of them have an autistic spectrum disorder, then it's best if SKIP is the only one outside our porch installation as our visitors arrive, and the rest of the travellers are playing on the porch.

In this case SKIP doesn't rush the students and their companions inside the installation but lets them take a look at what is going on inside through the doors and, particularly, the little windows.

When the visitors do this, the travellers – each one with their parcel, suitcase, bag or trunk beside them – can be seen within.

ACE is playing his guitar.

Outside, SKIP says welcoming words, like:

SKIP: Hi there. Welcome. They're waiting for the train. Go inside and join them if you like. They're friendly.

Second Scene

Each of the travellers is assigned a seat and an area on the installation porch. The travellers make the visitor(s) in the seats nearest to them feel comfortable, saying things like:

BELLE: Hi, I'm Belle.

She rings her bell.

BELLE: What's your name? I'm waiting for the train. Maybe you'd like to sit for a while and talk. Make yourself comfortable. This is my suitcase, my Blues Bag. In here are the things that I always want to take with me, wherever I go. What's in your Blues Bag, if you don't mind me asking?

Once all the visitors have been seated, and the basic introductions made (as in the example with BELLE above) SKIP blows his station master's whistle, waves his green flag, and we go into the song:

BIG JACK'S verse:

I hear a train a-coming
It's gonna take me away
I hear a train a-coming
It's gonna take me today

It's gonna take me home brother
Train gonna take me home
Gonna take me home sister
Train gonna take me home

It's gonna take me home mamma
Train gonna take me home
Gonna take me home, everybody now
Train's gonna take me home

BLUE BELLE's verse

I can hear the whistle blowin'
But I still can't see no train
I can hear the whistle blowin'
But I still can't see no train

It's gonna take me home brother, etc

Now the travellers take it in turns to introduce the visitor sitting next to them, and reveal what each is carrying in his or her luggage.

The order of introductions is:

LIGHTNIN'
BELLE
CHAMPION
LIGHTNIN' (AGAIN)
BIG JACK
BELLE (AGAIN)

This would go something like:

LIGHTNIN':   My name is (makes the sign) Lightnin'. Hello. I'd like to introduce you to Stephen. He's come along here today with Caroline. And can you guess what he's brought in his Blues Bag, the thing that he always takes with him wherever he goes?

CHAMPION: What's in his Blues Bag?

ACE produces the object of reference, or it might be something written or drawn on a card from within his visitor's Blues Bag.

ACE: It's a picture of his dog, Bobby.

BELLE: That's a great dog. I'd never leave that dog behind.
My name is Belle and I've got Donna sitting here with me. She's come along here today with Mrs Pritchard. And can you guess what she's brought in her Blues Bag, the thing that she always takes with her, wherever she goes?

CHAMPION: What's in her Blues Bag?

BELLE produces the object of reference, or whatever, from within her visitor's Blues Bag.

BELLE: It's her pink hat

BIG JACK: That's a great hat. I'd never leave that hat behind.
Hi, my name is Big Jack and I've got Donald sitting here with me. He's come along here today with Malcolm. Can you guess what he's brought in his Blues Bag, the thing that he always takes with him wherever he goes?

CHAMPION: What's in his Blues Bag?

BIG JACK produces the object of reference, or whatever, from within his visitor's Blues Bag.

BIG JACK: It's a Duplo block.

LIGHTNIN':   Duplo's great. I'd never leave Duplo behind.

And so on, with LIGHTNIN' introducing the next traveller and companion, with comments from CHAMPION, helped out by BIG JACK.

Then CHAMPION, helped by BIG JACK, introduces the fifth traveller and companion, with comments from BELLE and BIG JACK.

Finally BELLE introduces the sixth pair with comments from ACE and CHAMPION.

Third Scene

BIG JACK: It's a real pleasure to meet you all. Helps pass the time till that train comes.

He's interrupted by ACE'S guitar.

ACE: Big Jack, ain't you forgettin' someone?

BIG JACK: Sorry, stranger, go right ahead.

ACE half-sings his lines.

ACE: Hi everybody. My name is Ace, I like to play a little guitar from time to time.

He plays.

BELLE rings her bell.

BELLE: It was kind of you to tell us what's in your Blues Bags and I'd like to tell you what I've got in mine.

CHAMPION: What's in your Blues Bag, Belle?

Lights change.

BELLE carries her suitcase to the central position.

She unclasps first one, then the other of the catches, and begins to raise the lid.

Freeze.

Video A
Sound of fan.
Then fan fanning

Everyone gestures towards the screens.

ALL: Look! Look!

As the on-screen fan fans, BELLE distributes other fans to each of the six visitors and their companions.

Fanning music.

The travellers fan or encourage the companions to use the fans. The travellers always offer the visitors a choice: 'Would you like me to fan your hands, or the back of your neck? Or shall we just sit and watch?'

She sings:

Feel the wind on your face
Feel the wind in your hair
Feel the wind, feel the wind
Feel the wind everywhere

Feel the wind on your hands
Feel the wind in your hair
Feel the wind, feel the wind
Feel the wind everywhere

Feel the mist on your face
Feel the mist on your hair
Feel the mist, feel the mist
Feel the mist everywhere

Feel the wind on your neck
Feel the wind rock your chair
Feel the wind, feel the wind
Feel the wind everywhere

BELLE takes an atomiser from the case and walks about spraying a perfumed mist.

The fans are used to waft this about.

As the music dies away, the fans are collected up and returned to BELLE'S Blues Bag.

She returns her Blues Bag to its original position.

BELLE: And that's what (RINGS) Belle has got in her Blues Bag.

Lighting returns to general state.

Fourth Scene

ACE draws everyone's attention with his guitar and begins to descend from his ladder.

ACE: Thank you, Belle. It was kind of you to tell us what's in your Blues Bag and, in return, I'd like to tell you what I've got in mine.

CHAMPION: What's in your Blues Bag, Ace?

Lights change.

ACE carries his Blues Bag to the central area.

As he undoes the bag and starts to open it – freeze.

*Video B
First the sound, then images of a shaker shaking*

Everyone gestures towards the screens.

ALL: Look! Look!

CHAMPION, BELLE and BIG JACK hand out shakers amongst the visitors and their companions

ACE gets a groove going, and then comes in on guitar.

ACE'S Groove Song:

62

Shake that thing
C'mon and shake that thing
Shake that thing
C'mon and shake that thing
Shake that thing, shake that thing
We gonna shake that thing
We gonna shake that thing
Shake that thing ooh oo
Shake that thing ooh oo

Now you're in the groove

Now you're in the groove
Now you're in the groove
Now you're in the groove
You're in the groove, you're in the groove
You know you're in the groove
You know you're in the groove
You're in the groove ooh oo
You're in the groove ooh oo

Feel alright
C'mon and feel alright
Feel alright
C'mon and feel alright
Y'all feel alright, y'all feel alright
Y'all feel alright, y'all feel alright
You know you feel alright
We say you feel alright
Y'all feel alright ooh oo
Y'all feel alright ooh oo

After some variations, the groove slows and stops.

ACE collects up the shakers in his Blues Bag.

ACE: I have to take the rhythm with me. I can't leave the groove
                 behind. And that's what Ace has got in his Blues Bag.

ACE carries his Blues Bag back to its original position.
Lighting returns to general state.

Fifth Scene

CHAMPION: That was good, Ace!

ACE: Well thank you. But what I want to know is this, what's Big Jack got in that trunk of his?

CHAMPION: What's in your Blues Bag, Big Jack?

Lights change. BIG JACK drags his trunk to the central area, making the most of its weight.

BIG JACK reaches for the lid. He unfastens first one clasp, then the other.

He begins to raise the lid – and freezes.

Video C
First water sounds, then images of water.

ALL: Look! Look!

BIG JACK resumes, pulling the pump up out of the trunk. He pumps the handle and the water begins to flow, and continues to do so even when he leaves the handle and begins to splash the water around.

The other travellers hastily cover up the visitors with the towels set by their positions.

The travellers fill the washing bowls, each containing a sponge and a dollop of shampoo, at the pump and distribute to the visitors.

The travellers sing:
Verse (BIG JACK):
Water water flowing down
Water water all around
Water water falling from the skies
Water water can't believe my eyes

Chorus (ALL):
Have you felt the water fall?
Have you felt the water?
Have you felt the water fall?
Have you felt the water?
Water water falling on your hands
Feel the water falling on your hands.

BIG JACK: Bubbles.

CHAMPION: Soap.

BIG JACK: Bubbles.

CHAMPION: Soap.

BIG JACK: Bubbles.

CHAMPION: Soap.

They sing Soapsud Blues led by BIG JACK, and when they clap, they splash the bubbles around.

I got the Soapsud Blues (*clap clap*) (Soapsud Blues)
I got the Soapsud Blues (*clap clap*) (Soapsud Blues)
I got the Soapsud Blues (*clap clap*) (Soapsud Blues)

Stephen's got the Soapsud Blues (*clap clap*) (Soapsud Blues) etc

Donna's got the Soapsud Blues (*clap clap)* (Soapsud Blues) etc

...and so on until all the visitors have been named in a verse. Song ends with:

It's time to dry your hands (dry your hands) etc

That was the Soapsud Blues (Soapsud Blues) etc

The travellers remove the washing bowls, and help the companions to dry the visitors' hands, before carefully removing and folding the fluffy towels.

BIG JACK: And that's what (SIGN) Big Jack has got in his Blues Bag.

BIG JACK drags his case back to its original position.

The lighting returns to general state.

Sixth Scene

CHAMPION: You're very, very soapy good, Big Jack!

BIG JACK: Thank you, Champ. Now it must be your turn.

BELLE: Show us, Champ, what's that in your Blues Bag?

Lights change.

CHAMPION drags his trunk into the centre of the space. Lights fade to virtual blackout. He undoes first one catch and then the other. Then, as he starts to open the lid, stars shine from inside the BOX. He freezes.

Guitar harmonics, then CHAMPION unfreezes and reaches up to drag the stars down from the sky. Cue video of the starry sky and cicadas – Video D.

CHAMPION: Look! Look!

The other travellers distribute small cases to the visitors. The visitors open the case and find them to be filled with stars. They play with the stars.

(These small cases have an intense UV light source in their base. They are filled with tactile stars in UV colours.)

The visitors and their companions are encouraged to play with the light and the stars in the darkness.

The travellers sing:

On a dark, dark night
On a dark, dark night
You can feel alright
On a dark, dark night

When the stars come out
You can see the light
You can see the light
On a dark, dark night

CHAMPION raps:

On a dark night if there's no moonlight
And the suns out of sight, don't take a fright
On a dark night everything...will be alright

See the old moon rising
As the fireflies come out to play
Hear the crickets call to the whippoorwill
Feel your blues just melt away

On a dark, dark night
On a dark, dark night etc

Slowly CHAMPION closes the lid of his trunk, and, as he does so, the video image fades. The travellers make sure that all the UV boxes are turned off and shut tight.

CHAMPION: Good night stars. Good night.

Lighting returns to general state.

CHAMPION: And that's what (SIGN) Champion has got in his Blues Bag.

CHAMPION drags his case back to its original position.

Seventh Scene

ACE: There's still one Blues Bag left to open.

LIGHTNIN':   That's right, Ace.

CHAMPION: What's in your Blues Bag, Lightnin'?

Lights change.

LIGHTNIN' carries his case to the centre.

He undoes first one catch and then the other. It falls open – quite empty.

LIGHTNIN':   There's nothing in my Blues Bag. That's why I need this...

He produces his video camera.

LIGHTNIN':   My camera.

BELLE: What's that for?

LIGHTNIN':   To take pictures of my friends, so that I can remember
                      them, wherever I go.

TRAVELLERS: That's me! Look!

Video E (live)
Pan over three of the travellers.

LIGHTNIN':   And now I've got some new friends I met today.

*LIGHTNIN' takes the video camera around. He is accompanied by SKIP who
provides a pool of light with his railway lantern.*

We see large close-ups of the travellers projected across the two screens.

CHAMPION: That's me.

LIGHTNIN':   Yes, Champ. And that's my friend Belle.

*We begin to include live images of the visitors, with the image of the visitor
LIGHTNIN' has been teamed up with coming first.*

*As the travellers see the video image of each visitor come up on the screens, they
go into the naming song for that visitor.*

The order is:
ACE sings to the tune of Feel the Wind
JACK sings to the tune of I Hear a Train a Comin'
BELLE sings to the tune of Soapsud Blues
CHAMP sings to the tune of Shake That Thing

JACK sings to the tune of Water, Water
BELLE sings to the tune of Dark, Dark Night

LIGHTNIN':   I'd like to take all these pictures, and put them in my Blues Bag, so that I will remember you, wherever I go.

CHAMPION: Yeah, Lightnin'. That's right.

LIGHTNIN' puts his camera in the case and closes the lid.

LIGHTNIN':   So that's what (SIGN) Lightnin' has got in his Blues Bag.

He returns the case to its original position.

Eighth Scene

We hear the sound of a train whistle far off in the distance.

Then the train whistle is heard again – closer this time.

BELLE: It's the train.

Video F
Of the train arriving and smoke. Add real smoke machine smoke.

BIG JACK: Time for us to go.

Travellers mill about.

Each of the travellers repeats to their visitor, 'Time for us to go,' and individually thanks the companions and the visitors for the time they have spent together, along the following lines:

BELLE: It's been wonderful to meet you Donna, and you too Mrs Pritchard. I'll never forget the things we've shared today. I'd like to give you a small present, something to put in your Blues Bag. Maybe, after we've gone, when you look at this, you'll think about us and remember the good times we've had.

BELLE gives each of her two visitors a photo of the travellers (or a fan if they are vision-impaired)

ALL: I'd like to give you a small present, something to put in your Blues Bag. Maybe, after we've gone, when you look at this you'll think about us and remember the good times we've had.

The train whistle blows once more.

BIG JACK: Time to get our things on the train.

They carry, and help one another to carry, the pieces of luggage off the porch, and as they do they sing:

Verse:
Well we're waitin' at the station
Seems like we bin here since creation
But there's no time for hesitation
Got to get on board

Chorus:
Here comes the train
Here comes the train
Here comes the train
Got to get on board

Verse:
It's really quite peculiar
Sayin' so long to yer
But sing glory hallelujah
Got to get on board

Chorus repeat

Verse:
We gotta say goodbye to you
And to you and you and you
But right now you know it's true
We got to get on board

Chorus repeat

Verse:
Well there ain't no way of knowing
Exactly where we're going
But when you hear the whistle blowin'
Got to get board

Chorus repeat, during which the travellers stick their heads through the window holes.

Now the travellers make their way out of the porch installation, and line up outside the main entrance, waving goodbye and signing thank you to the departing visitors and their companions.

Song:

Did we say that you're looking fine
Did we stay you're just like sunshine
Did we say the stars shine from your eyes
We don't ever want to say goodbye
We don't ever want to say goodbye

Did we say you've all been oh so good
Did we say we'd stay here if we could
Did we say that we don't want to cry
We don't ever want to say goodbye
We don't ever want to say goodbye

If everyone is ambulant, they may all have left by the time we come to the end of the lyric. If there is a great deal of hoisting to be done, however, then the music should continue, while we help with getting people comfortably back into their wheelchairs and on their way.

As the final visitors depart, the whistle blows once more, the crossing bells clang and we hear the sound of the train pulling out as the travellers wave a final goodbye.

END

Blue 2006
Photo: Patrick Baldwin

Oily Cart

Blue 2006
Photo: Patrick Baldwin

Baby Balloon 2007
Photo: Patrick Baldwin

Oily Cart

Ring A Ding Ding 2011
Photo: Amanda Webb

Watch Oily Cart with wonder and admiration.
Lyn Gardner *The Guardian*

Something in the Air 2009
Photo: Nik Mackey

Big Balloon 2006
Photo: Edgar de Oliveira

Hippity Hop 2004
Photo: Amanda Webb

Dinner Ladies from Outer Space 1992
Photo: Andrew McDiarmid

Knock, Knock! Who's There? 2000
Photo: Jonathan Stockbridge

They were utterly captivated, the performance was so
flexible the players were able to accommodate each child's
needs. The live music was beautiful, the performers all sang
so well and the ambience was so loving, none of us wanted
to leave. *Audience feedback*

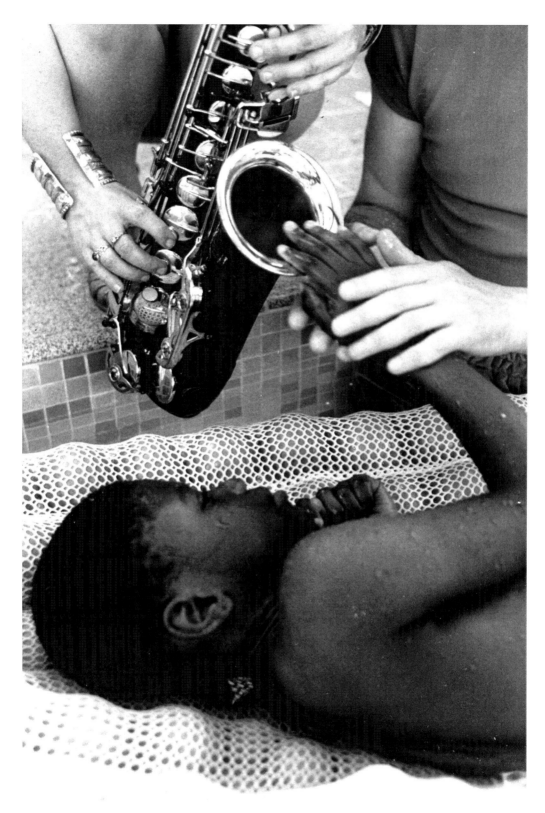

Bubbles 1997
Photo: Paul Harris

Oily Cart

Conference of the Birds 2004
Photo: Amanda Webb

A Peck of Pickled
Pepper 1998
Photo: Amanda Webb

Under Your Hat 2001
Photo: Amanda Webb

A ticket to an Oily
Cart show is like
an 'open sesame'
to an irresistible
playground for the
imagination and
the senses.
Mary Brennan
The Herald

Drum 2010
Photo: Patrick Baldwin

Baby Balloon 2007
Photo: Patrick Baldwin

Oily Cart

Dreams and Secrets 2000
Photo: Tony Kyriacou

Crystal showers through silver colanders
catch the triple light
as glitter balls rain on water.
The little boy stands by the poolside,
his eyes shimmering with music,
smiles of splashes
as the gong strikes laughter.
Aoife Mannix

Waving 2001
Photo: Andrew McDiarmid

Oily Cart

Jumpin' Beans 2002
Photo: Tim Webb

Play and its importance in life and art is at the heart of this intimate, low key production, which celebrates the transforming powers of the imagination. Kate Stratton *TIME OUT*

Drum 2010
Photo: Patrick Baldwin

Oily Cart

Boing 2002
Photo: Patrick Baldwin

Oily Cart

Words cannot capture or describe a unique performance that all our pupils related to in their own way. The expressions of delight and joy on all the pupils faces I will never forget. A truly magical experience. *Kilton Thorpe School*

Blue: a suggested timetable for a one-day visit

All sessions are 50 minutes long. A maximum of six young people and six companions can fit into our porch installation, a total of twelve spectators.

Any other observers must be seated outside the porch installation, except by very special arrangement.

We are only able to perform a maximum of four sessions per day.

It is possible to have any combination of PMLD [profound and multiple learning disabilities] and ASD [autism spectrum disorder] sessions during the day, but it is desirable for the ASD work to take place in the latter part of a visit, so that the ASD students have plenty of opportunity to visit the installation before they actually join us for a performance.

What follows is only a serving suggestion:

8.00-10.00	Get-in and fit up
10.00-10.50	First PMLD session (for up to 6 young people with PMLD and their carers)
10.50-11.00	Re-set
11.00-11.50	Second PMLD session
11.50-12.00	Re-set
12.00-13.00.	Lunch (ASD students could visit, even have their sandwiches on the set)
13.00-13.50	First ASD session (for up to six young people with ASD and their carers)
13.50-14.00	Re-set
14.00-14.50	Second ASD session
15.00-15.15	The Bus Busk (an all-singin', all playin', all dancin' farewell to the whole school as they get onto their buses and leave for home.)

Making *Baby Balloon*

In *Baby Balloon* (2006), a giant balloon starts to glow. Then, two playful dancers emerge from inside and invite the audience to explore the colours, music and textures of their airy world.

For each highly interactive performance, ten babies [aged between six months and two years old] and their carers entered a magical world of balloons. An exploration of the senses of touch, sound, smell, taste and sight, *Baby Balloon* was a perfect introduction to the enchantment of theatre for young children.

The show toured venues around the UK and in Europe in 2006, 2007 and 2008.

Writer and director Tim Webb, designer Claire de Loon and musical director Max Reinhardt talked to Mark Brown about the making of the show.

Tim Webb
Writing and directing *Baby Balloon*

Like a lot of things with Oily Cart, there's an influence from our work with kids who have special needs, where necessity is the mother of invention. We discovered that there were things in the special needs shows that would apply to other audiences and other forms of theatre. A lot of the things that we did in *Baby Balloon* came out of our experience of doing shows for kids with special educational needs and profound and multiple learning disabilities (PMLD); shows like *Conference of the Birds* (2004) and *Blue* (2006).

We realised with the shows for PMLD children that we could engage an audience that didn't have any verbal language. Then we thought, 'We've seen these other guys around who don't have much verbal language – children under two.' That was the starting point for *Baby Balloon*; it gave us the key to a door we'd been looking to unlock for a long time, work for the very young.

The other thing we took from the special needs shows into *Baby Balloon* was the importance of dealing with everyone in the room. There are always going to be adults present. In the special needs shows, there will be adults, whether they're parents or teachers, accompanying children with, for example, an autistic spectrum disorder. The children will be paying those adults a lot of attention, because they're very significant people in their lives. If the adults' shoulders are all hunched with tension or they're yawning with boredom, it's going to have an effect on the kids. So you have to carry everybody with you. And anyway, isn't that a good thing? I always think, if you're the parent of a child with a severe disability or you're teaching in a school for kids with severe learning disabilities, you're carrying a heavy load, you're entitled to some theatrical fun too.

We applied many of the same principles to *Baby Balloon*. The big difference is that what are called 'neurotypical' babies and toddlers react with astonishing speed compared with an audience of people with severe learning disabilities.

There's no narrative in *Baby Balloon*, but the strategy was that the audience would start off as if looking through a fourth wall, and the action starts to penetrate the fourth wall. Balloons come out of the big balloon and go into the audience, and the audience realise that you can touch and play with these things. This gives rise to a lot of playing, back and forth across the fourth wall, until the bubbles come out of the big inflatable balloon and draw the children and everybody else towards and, eventually, inside the big balloon. Once inside, they eat the oranges and are in an atmosphere that's very intimate, pervaded by smells and the warmth of other people's bodies. So you were taken from the position of being an objective spectator to being a participant in an all-pervasive world.

We were experimenting. In that show, we ended up leaving the audience to play with the props and materials we'd introduced. In other shows, we've done it the other way round: we started off letting them play, for example in the under-twos version of *Jumpin' Beans* (2002). In that show they played with the bouncy, boingy objects, then the characters wandered in and took them on a more structured adventure. Both ways of doing it work.

We've figured out that there has to be a sort of antechamber to the main event in our shows. You have to let people become comfortable, find their bearings and settle down. Then they'll be prepared to go off on a journey with you. I'd say, even though *Baby Balloon* has no narrative, the audience was taken on a journey. The wonderful thing about being a six-month-old baby is that you can just glory in whatever's coming along in sensory terms.

There are two notable things about the process of making *Baby Balloon*. One is that there never was a script. I amused Max greatly, because we got everyone into the rehearsal room for what was supposedly going to be the read through. He was surprised when I banged a folder on the desk and he said, 'What you got in there then?' When I opened it up, there was nothing inside it, because nothing existed. In the end, the stage manager made a props list and a cue list, and that's as close to a script for *Baby Balloon* as we got.

The other thing is that we rehearsed it in an amazingly short period of time. We usually have five weeks. In this case, because of restrictions on people's availability, we'd be rehearsing for just a couple of hours in an evening. We did that for about a week. Then we went to Brussels, to an art centre we were going to be working in. At that point, another musician joined us. It was all a bit hair-raising, but what we had – and I would say this is a key thing with Oily Cart shows – was a strong concept to work with.

I had this idea of the audience starting off looking at the inflatable pod objectively, but then being drawn into a sensory totality. We had this lovely inflatable from the outset, and an array of balloon-type material. So, we knew it was going to be strong conceptually. It was a case of getting the performers to be confident about working with the audiences and the structure and running order of the show.

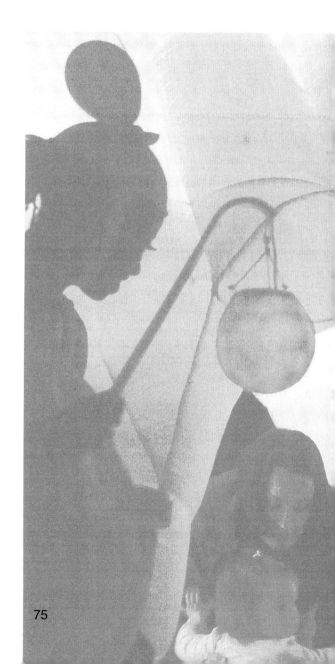

Claire de Loon
Designing *Baby Balloon*

Designing theatre for babies and toddlers is a similar challenge to designing shows for children and young people with disabilities in the sense that you're dealing with an audience who are experiencing something that's challenging to them. They're not used to it. They're going into a strange space, and they're nervous. Little children can easily be frightened. So we have to make the space very welcoming.

Seating arrangements are always an issue with baby and toddler shows. With *Baby Balloon* we were moving the audience around. They'd start off sitting on the floor, on a carpet, and then they'd start moving about a bit, in that they are being given sensory things to join in with. Then they have to get up and go into the balloon. It's that inside-outside thing. You've got two different environments, the open one and the enclosed, very intimate one. Finally, when you come back out, you come into a transformed open environment. So there are in effect three different spaces, and the way you moved around them was interesting.

Lighting is very important to design, of course. Tim is very good on lighting, and usually takes the lead where that is concerned. We also work with various lighting designers. Good lighting designers add so much, it's really important. You can see that they've really understood what you're trying to do, and they enhance it.

In terms of the aesthetic, if you have high production standards, people appreciate it. When we opened *Baby Balloon*, it was in the Pantalone arts centre in Brussels. The people there were just so appreciative. They clapped and clapped, and wrote all sorts of things about the poetry of it. They just appreciated every aspect of it.

We commissioned [inflatable designer and maker] Rachel James to make the pod itself. The inflatable was the starting point for the whole thing. We've had two collaborations with Rachel [*Jumpin' Beans* and *Conference of the Birds*]. She's a very creative designer. Inflatables are also very practical for touring.

We decided to commission her to make an inflatable for the show, and we would then make the whole thing about inflatables; about air, balloons and things floating. We told her that we wanted a space that you could go inside and that it would be a giant balloon, and that it should be white so that we could change the colour. We said that it would have to have a hole at the end so that people could look in, as well as an opening through which you came in and out. Audience size was determined by how many people we could squeeze into the pod.

We had the pod at the start of rehearsals, which was very important. One of the big things we struggle with is the question of how much of the show you have at the start of rehearsals. You need your puppets and your set, but if it's too finished, you can't adjust it to the ideas that come out of rehearsals. With *Baby Balloon* we needed to have the pod from the outset.

Where colour is concerned, people have this idea that children's things have to be multicoloured. I don't come at it from that angle at all. I think that's all wrong, really. You just have to choose your colour palette, and try to make it appropriate for the theme of the show. You should try to be as economical as possible in whatever you're doing. The monochrome is the strongest, but if the show becomes too monochrome, then it's not child-friendly. It's a question of finding the right balance.

Another example would be the show *If All the World were Paper*, in which we started out in black and white, then introduced blue, and we ended up in colour. That was about Paper Girl's journey, and her becoming more and more open to new ideas.

As with all shows for these very young audiences, it was important that *Baby Balloon* allowed for free play. The design is part of that. We had the treasure baskets at the end, with lights inside. These design elements help to enhance the free play within the shows.

Max Reinhardt
Making music for *Baby Balloon*

Tim [Webb] is always aware of stuff I do, musically, outside the Oily Cart. He knew that I was part of this strange group I still work with some-times, that was all about combining a DJ with a live musician. So when he was out in Belgium at the Pantalone arts centre – which is an important Flemish arts centre, where they are pretty avant-garde in their thinking, and where we were going to premiere *Baby Balloon* – he told them we would put a live musician together with me in the role of improvising DJ.

So that was the plan on paper. Then we began to think about which musician we would get to join us. The sort of music we would have in the show hadn't really been considered.

I'd worked in the past with this amazing cellist, Ernst Reijsiger, who's from The Netherlands. I met him at a jazz festival in Istanbul. One of the things that happens at good jazz festivals is that everybody plays with everybody else at every level. After he'd been on in this club in Istanbul, I and some other people from England were doing our kind of DJ/live musician thing and he said, 'I really love this, can I join in?' At the time he was in a band with a Senegalese percussionist. So they both joined in and we jammed together, and every-body had a great time.

Afterwards he said to me, 'I'd love to do more things with you.' He came over to London and we did some stuff together. So I knew that I could phone Ernst up, and The Netherlands isn't far from Brussels. Maybe he'd do it. Or maybe he'd be far too expensive, because he's probably the number one jazz cellist in the world. Plus, he does classical and contemporary classical work. He seems to work non-stop.

But he really loved the idea and in particular the idea of doing work for babies. We didn't really know what collaborating with him on this project would be like. I'd worked with him in very different contexts, of course, and Tim knew his work and thought he was a genius. It all looked good. In fact, we were delighted that one of our arcane hero figures was coming to work with us. However, he couldn't come to any of the rehearsals in London.

Remember, this is a dance show for babies. Babies, balloons, dance, improvising music – it sounds so 60s! Anyway, not only could our musician not come to London, but our choreographer couldn't come to Brussels!

Around this time, I was getting into this sampling programme called Ableton Live, on which you can write stuff, put it into the system and then play with it. It's got a million effects, and you can do it all live. I was in love with this thing so I wanted to write some electronica for *Baby Balloon*. I was always thinking as I wrote the tracks, 'Ernst is going to improvise over this so I need to leave lots of space for him.'

I had to sell everyone the idea that I would be using this sampling programme instead of DJ decks. However, everybody liked the way that the programme allowed the music to mutate and go faster and slower. The possibilities seemed boundless.

The other thing we wanted to do was sample balloon sounds. I had live balloon sounds in the show but I also sampled some intricate balloonery.

By the time we went to Brussels, we had all the musical numbers sorted. Likewise with the action of the show. It doesn't really have a narrative but it is a sequence of routines.

Add to that the fact that we were about to do *Blue*, for which I had rediscovered my harmonica. So I had all my music ready to go, plus the harmonica, and other little gadgets and recognisable instruments that I could play.

We started work in Brussels without the choreographer but with dancers knowing the choreography she'd worked out with them in London. The London rehearsal process had been quite an interesting way of working. On each day of rehearsals the choreographer would tell me what she was planning to do the following day or in two days' time so that I could do music for it. Then on the rehearsal room floor it would change a bit.

When we got to Brussels it was Ernst who, just by playing along with it, changed it completely. He completely transformed the way I thought about it. Sometimes he'd do contemporary classical things, sometimes he didn't necessarily do the jazz things I thought he was going to do but then he would do them at a different part of the show.

At one point in the music, where I'd written it as a kind of mathematical formula with an extra note added every 16 bars, he turned it into almost a holy chant. It became really quite religious and ritualistic. That's the music that we played when the children's faces appear on the balloon.

It was a non-stop experiment. We carried on changing as it went on, not only in rehearsals in Brussels but during the two weeks of the show. It really was an improvised show, musically. It was truly a very different and wonderful way of working, which we hadn't done before and haven't done since.

After Brussels, the show became something that would have to tour for months at a time without Ernst and mostly without me. I had a recording of the music from Brussels because Pantalone had made a multi-microphone recording of it, so it was quite high quality. Back in London, I worked with an extremely happening younger jazzer called Finn Peters, who knew Ernst and Tim from way back. Between us we cut the Pantalone recording into backing tracks that we'd use in the show. Also, Finn used the Ableton Live programme to mutate things and play sax and flute over them as well. This second version of the show was still improvised, musically, but we were improvising on the basis of the first version in Brussels. You could still hear bits of Ernst. On later tours Tunde Jegede replaced Finn and played cello and kora.

The first time we did a show for babies [*Jumpin' Beans*, 2002], we went quite pretty and placid with the music. But with *Baby Balloon* there were absolutely no barriers.

Audience feedback for *Baby Balloon* (2006) at Pantalone Art House in Brussels

Wonderfully beautiful! Good balance between observing and participating. I would never have believed the smallest ones could be attentive for such a long time.

Great show full of suprises, poetry, colour, music. They loved it!

What an adventure! Perfect!

Great! When are you coming again? You have contagious creativity!!!

A superb performance, combining the five senses with beautiful poetry. Truly delightful!

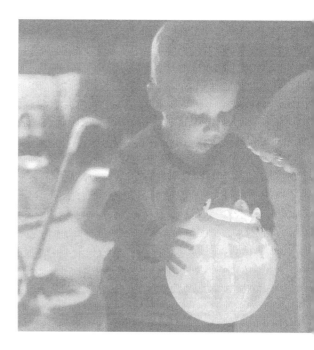

Review

The following review of *Baby Balloon*, by Mary Brennan, appeared in *The Herald* on February 9, 2007.

 ticket to an Oily Cart show is like an 'open sesame' to an irresistible playground for the imagination and the senses.

And though Baby Balloon is intended for toddlers – specifically those aged two and under – the sheer invention that's at work, or rather at play, is every bit as inspiring for adults. The fun begins as soon as you enter the studio: the air is full of tweet-tweetering birdsongs, and there's a red carpet with wee beanbags for toddlers and parents to loll on. Upstage, a huge pod-cum-hot-air balloon is lying on its side.

This pod will soon produce a breezy individual in stripy socks, stripy jersey and short, balloon-baggy dungarees. Everything about her (Keiko Hewitt-Teale) just says 'playmate'. The way she makes friendly eye contact with the babies, grins genially at the two-year-olds and generally paves the way for a touchy-feely adventure – that even incorporates taste and smell – is beautifully gauged and reassuring. Together with Anthea Lewis – and abetted by musician Max Reinhardt, with Edgar de Olivera supplying video – she draws us into a magical realm of colours and sounds where balloons fly high, the pod itself changes colours when touched and a trail of bubbles is a Pied Piper lure to lead tinies inside for a tea ceremony. (Okay, slice of orange.) As ever, there's a hugely sophisticated structure and back-up to what seems simplicity itself.

I'm tempted to describe the video projections and colour washes as blissful psychedelia for tots. But then add in the interactive element where toddlers get to be hands-on curious, to squish, blow, scrunch and sniff objects tied in to the on-stage larks, and you soon appreciate how Baby Balloon is one of the jolliest informal learning experiences any tot could wish for.

Making *Ring a Ding Ding*

Ring a Ding Ding (2011) is an epic, though tiny, table-top voyage of discovery, where the young audience are invited to get their fingers and noses in the action. An immersive, interactive and multisensory show, it was made for children aged three to six and their families.

Writer and director Tim Webb, designer Claire de Loon and musical director Max Reinhardt talk to Mark Brown about the making of the show.

Tim Webb
Writing and directing *Ring a Ding Ding*

Ring a Ding Ding fits in a slot that's been a key part of Oily Cart's strategy over the past five or six years, which is to do a Christmas run of a show, followed by a national tour. These shows have been for two to six-year-olds or three to six-year-olds.

In this show – in addition to the things you might expect in a show, such as story and character – the audience are going to be delighted by lots of chances to intervene in the action and lots of opportunities to talk to the characters and help them with their problems. Also, there are the multisensory pleasures you quite often associate with Oily Cart shows, like getting sprayed with water or finding yourself under falling bubbles. These young audiences are very fruitful to work for. We're always able to include several of our obsessions in one package.

My original idea for *Ring a Ding Ding* was that it would be great if you were watching a show in which you had your fingers on the stage and your nose in the scenery. The concept was that everyone would have a front row seat, and the show would, in effect, swing round to them. The actors are about 50 centimetres away from the children most of the time. I think that concept has really worked.

The kids are so focused, so involved and so engaged that it's just bloody delightful. We've had a similar proximity of actors to audience in shows for babies and toddlers, but this is the closest we've brought children to the action in shows for threes to sixes.

The other thing the children do, and it's great that they do it (we weren't sure if they would), is help to turn the turntable. They love doing it. In fact, sometimes the problem is that they won't stop doing it! We did have a wooden peg that the stage manager could use to stop the turntable going round, but one unruly South London school did away with that. So now we have a tungsten steel peg.

With Oily Cart we've developed ways of getting kids to stop doing things we'd rather they didn't do without getting all disciplinarian about it. Partly it's about distracting them by giving them something more interesting to see or do, and partly it's about the actors we cast in the shows. If you have someone sounding teacherly, or like a policeman, it ruins the whole thing, I think.

One of the great things about theatre – and we've found this working in Special Needs schools, particularly – is that you're not like any of the authority figures the children have encountered before. You're not a parent who's trying to get them to do the right thing, or a teacher who's trying to teach them something, or a policeman who's trying to stop them from doing something naughty.

In fact, more often than not, the children feel that they know more than the characters do. It's always important to empower the kids in one way or another. One way to do that is to have adults who don't have a clue what they are doing.

In *Ring a Ding Ding*, Griff [Fender] plays a series of characters, none of whom knows anything really. For example, first of all he's the dog. This dog runs round in circles, chasing its own tail. That's all it knows how to do. He's also the milkman, but he only knows how to go left. Then he's the captain of a ship that does tours of the bay, but it's always the same way round the bay. At the end of the show he realises that his ship will also do reverse.

Claire [de Loon] and Max [Reinhardt] and I were talking about How Long is a Piece of String? being our favourite Oily Cart show in this genre. We think *Ring a Ding Ding* is up there with it.

The shows start off with me writing a script, and Claire's usually at the other end of the table doing the design. I'll bounce ideas off her and she'll make suggestions. Quite often a major concept in the show comes from her. In How Long is a Piece of String? for example, the idea of a whole bunch of babies being missing came from her, and it's the plot motor.

With *Ring a Ding Ding*, I was worried that the plot motor just seemed to be that this dog stops chasing its own tail and just runs away. I thought, 'Cor blimey, this is a bit thin!' But it seems to have worked. It's an issue that the children, even the five and six-year-olds, are engaged with. They want the dog to be found. Everyone's in despair, they don't know where to turn. Then, off in the corner of the theatre you hear, 'Woof woof woof', and it's a case of 'there's your dog, go and get him'. It's a very simple issue but it's crucial to the success of the show.

With this sort of show, you have to, somehow, get an issue that a two-year-old can understand, as well as the older children. At the Unicorn [Theatre in London] when the dog ran away, one kid burst into tears. It was too heavy emotionally for this little boy. I thought, 'This is such a manky dog he should be celebrating!'

There's a moment when the dog comes out on a motor bike. The kids love that – but then so do the adults. You'd have to be pretty po-faced not to dig a dog on a motorbike!

Claire de Loon
Designing *Ring a Ding Ding*

With this show we have a circular set and a whole series of things that go round and round. At the centre of the set is a revolving play board and in the middle of it is a mast with arms coming off it, which is a bit like a children's merry-go-round at the funfair.

The mast has emblems on it: it has the sun in the middle and the Earth and the moon go round the sun. We also hang pieces of scenery off the rotating arms. This gives the set height: the children are not just seeing things at eye level – which in this case is very low – they're also seeing things above them.

The children are also seeing things all around them. The actors come out from the middle, from under the play board and run around the outside. In addition to that, we've got [musician] George [Panda] on his tricycle, playing his musical instruments, and he's riding around on the outside of everything. So everything's going round and round at all different levels.

We're using the theatre space so that the audience has things coming from a distance, then being up close. You've got the actors, who are big, and then you have little puppets of the same characters that the actors are playing.

Two of the vehicles for the puppets were made by South African wire worker Mogothi. We made the other vehicles and the puppets, all in the same style.

The way that came about is that years ago I saw an exhibition at the Bethnal Green Museum of Childhood [in London] which had wire toys from Zimbabwe. They were really beautiful things, made by children. They are kinetic toys. You push them along, and the wheels go round, and that makes the legs go up and down and the figures seem to be pedalling. We've used that idea in quite a few shows.

I'd been in touch with Mia van Zyl, who had been a design assistant with Oily Cart in the past, and who'd moved back to South Africa. I just thought, on this show perhaps she could organise for some original wire work to be done for us in South Africa. And she did! That's the thing about the internet: you can communicate with people quickly, you can send designs, and this wonderful person understood what it was we wanted and was able to find the maker and explain to him exactly what it was we wanted.

In keeping with the theme of the show, all the props and puppets are made from recycled materials. The costumes are similar. A lot of them are made from old Oily Cart costumes.

It's a multicoloured aesthetic because of the recycling theme. We're using a lot of drinks cans, commercial packaging and a lot of cheap plastic things that are used in Africa. Because it has all this colour, I tried to keep everything else as monochrome as possible so that it isn't all multicoloured everywhere. Philip Prowse [designer and director at the Citizens Theatre, Glasgow, 1970-2004] was my teacher; he taught me to be as economical with the colours as possible.

The set is basically white and yellow. The merry-go-round in the middle is yellow. Everything is made to look old and used, but the bright colours stand out.

It's great to have the lovely old tricycle in the show. It was one of the earliest things we invested in for Oily Cart. It's sort of emotional to bring it back into a show.

Our way of working, in which we have a theme and then develop a whole series of ideas that are consistent with that theme, works very well for us. But when you start developing all these ideas, you have to sort out what you really need.

I can't stress enough the importance to our work of the cast. We try to ensure that our teams always include men and women, a range of ages and a range of ethnicities. That's really important to us. It's very unusual for us to have an all-white cast, for instance. We have that very occasionally but it's through default, because we haven't been able to get an ethnically diverse cast. A lot of children's theatre is being made by young white people, and that's not what we want to put on stage – we want to reflect on-stage the society around us.

Max Reinhardt
Making music for *Ring a Ding Ding*

There are certain themes that you associate with different periods of Oily Cart. The voyage is important at the moment. It hasn't always been important, but it is now. *Ring a Ding Ding* is one of those shows.

It's a really interesting show for me, for a number of reasons. If we take it right back to early 2011, we asked ourselves, 'What's the music like in *Ring a Ding Ding*?' and we came up with the answer, 'Obviously it's ring a ding ding music!' So that was simple.

I'd been listening to a female French musician, Colleen Schott, who plays with bell music and various electronic ways of using it. I said, 'Maybe we ought to have lots of bells on the set but no dedicated musicians, just those bells and backing tracks made out of bell sounds.' I don't even know if Tim and Claire remember that, because it isn't what we did in the end, because more interesting things happened.

Tim and Claire were working on the idea that *Ring a Ding Ding* was a ring thing rather than a bell thing. It was all about going round and round, which meant recycling, amongst other things. It meant round and round in every conceivable way. It is very much one of those shows in which we are obsessively immersed in the concept, the world of ring.

As Claire became interested in Southern African wire toys, we started to think, 'Maybe the music's Southern African.' I was very comfortable with that, because I've been very involved with South African music, whether it's been playing it as a DJ or actually performing it, for a couple of decades now.

So I was thinking, 'This is all going to sound a bit Zulu and township.' Then I thought, 'How am I going to make it sound 'ringy'?' The answer lay with a guy we know called Jamie Linwood, who's a genius at making musical instruments. Jamie has a PhD in pitched percussion; I found him via the

OILY CART – ALL SORTS OF THEATRE FOR ALL SORTS OF KIDS

musical instrument making department at East London University. He made the drum for *Drum* (2010), and various instruments that play themselves in the water for our water shows.

As I was still in the *Drum* zone [the show was being performed in different versions throughout 2011], I thought we could probably use the percussionist we had on that show to play the instruments we were about to invent. His name is George Panda and he is from Sierra Leone and he was truly excellent at playing the Ghanaian balafon we had in *Drum*. So I thought, 'As long as George can hit things, we'll be alright.' Then I had to work with Jamie on aspects like what kind of scales the instruments were going to play and what they were going to look like.

Tim or Claire remembered the old ice cream tricycle, which is possibly from the 40s or 50s. We bought it in the early eighties and featured it in the first Oily Cart summer park show. This was a show called Grease (1982), and it was all about a dirty hamburger stand. So, we had thrown the ice cream fridge [which was attached to the tricycle] away, and put in its place this hamburger stand that you could cycle round the park. The trike's been in a couple of shows since, for example, it was in a show for Special Needs schools called *Funky Philharmonic* (1991).

Tim and Claire said, 'While you're asking Jamie to build all these instruments, can you make sure that they'll all fit on this tricycle? Because, if possible, we'd like the trike cycled round and round the outside of the performance and seating area.' Jamie loved that idea more than anything else I said to him, because he, too, is an eccentric.

We started thinking about the instruments. We knew they had to be made from recycled material. We were thinking of a Congolese band called Konono No1, who did an album called *Congotronics* on which they play homemade likembes (Congolese thumb pianos) and metallic marimbas that they strike, and a glorious metallic buzzing sound issues forth. We thought that might sound a bit like bells. So Jamie started to cut up a car chassis to make one of those marimba-like things.

Then, thinking *Tubular Bells* [the 1973 album by Mike Oldfield], we asked Jamie to make instruments out of scaffolding pipes. And, finding that his gamelan was boingy rather than ringy, Jamie said he wanted to make something that was halfway between a steelpan and a gamelan. He made some of these and they looked a bit like flying saucers.

Finally, there was a fourth instrument. It's an interesting thing. It's got a saddle that you sit on, and it's got eight pipes on the front that you hit.

So we had our four instruments but there were still a number of problems. Jamie wanted to know how we wanted the instruments tuned. We agreed on pentatonic. Then we agreed the notes.

I didn't know whether I could learn to play these instruments and write the music on them. There was no point writing it on anything else. And anyway that is generally how I work – I write the music on the instruments we're going to be using in the show, although I know that the musician who's going to be playing it can play it better than me.

I went to where Jamie lives in the Cotswolds and collected all the instruments. I worked on them for a week to see what would happen. Tim had sent me the script with all the lyrics, which was loved.

I wrote the music and thought the backing vamps did all sound a bit similar, but I assumed that was just because I wasn't very good at playing the instruments and, besides, I knew that George's percussive skills would really make it take off. Sure enough, once he accepted that he really would have to make these strange tubes ring and that there was no drum anywhere in the building, George was quite happy. He did a beautiful job of turning my scratch arrangements into really brilliant music.

Much of the music was a bit high for my voice and as you could only play the instruments in one key, no transposing was possible. But I thought that might be good for Elayce [Ismail] and Alicia [McKenzie], the two women singers in the show, and I knew Griff's golden voice would find its own way through

Audience feedback for
Ring a Ding Ding (2011)

Totally age-appropriate, fantastic multisensory show. Again (as with all Oily Cart productions) very, very high production values, stunning design, incredibly evocative music, strong performances and just the right balance of interaction for the young audience.

Makes me want to cry! It's so good!

A rich experience, with fabulous care, expertise and attention to detail in design, construction, conception and delivery. Beautiful (as always).

It was perfectly timed to grasp their attention the whole way through. The story was beautiful and was turned into a magic event by the actors. What a beautiful show to be enjoyed not only by the children but also by the adults.

Review

The following review of *Ring a Ding Ding* by Caroline McGinn appeared in *Time Out* on December 15, 2011.

Oily Cart creates the kind of children's shows that you want to take home and treasure forever. Its latest intimate epic for three to six-year-olds is a simple story, about a girl who loses her dog and goes to the moon to find him. But it's the way they tell them that make Oily Cart's stories so special.

This one chases its own tail delightfully in the round, where it is presented with extraordinary charm and artistry by three engaging performers, a musician who circles proceedings on his amazing melodic tricycle and a convoy of charmingly homemade puppets, bicycles, milk floats, boats and motorbikes.

This is streets ahead of most children's shows – and, in its deft use of promenade, it leaves many adult theatre companies for dust. Oily Cart's theatre space is also a playground, where pre-schoolers push their way through chiming bell-laden hoops, then sit quietly around the circular stage and help turn it round and round with their hands.

You'd imagine it would be chaos: instead, the audience is hooked, entranced and utterly persuaded to imagine themselves into the story. Quite simply, Oily Cart makes art for small children: a beguiling aesthetic experience, scaled to fit their curious world and perfectly designed to make them happy.

The Casts

How do the performers in Oily Cart shows fit into the company's unique aesthetic? It is a question that has, no doubt, been asked many times, of many people. Here, through a series of six interviews with cast members from the recent and distant past, we gain insights into how actors and, in one case, an aerial artist helped to make six particular shows and share a variety of memories of the Oily Cart collaborative method, both on-stage and off.

Pool Piece 2009 Photo: Jesus Gamon

Interview with Sjaak van der Bent

Performer with Oily Cart, 1998-2008

Please describe the process of preparation for *Pool Piece* (2008)

As part of the research for the show about twenty artists were selected to get together and work on different multisensory aspects that might be used. There were some visual artists, sound artists, and people with backgrounds working in schools for kids with disabilities. We brainstormed ideas on how *Pool Piece* might work.

This was a great experience. It was very free. From this process we devised a short show for kids with learning disabilities, and we also did a show for older people with Alzheimer's disease. It was very interesting to see how the multisensory approach could work for both young children and elderly people. It was amazing – we did some really funny things and some very interesting things as well.

We developed *Pool Piece* through workshops. A poet did a workshop, which was about words, and also about patterns. A lot of people with learning disabilities or Alzheimer's might not understand certain things, linguistically, so the workshop was about the relationships between sounds, words and patterns, and how we use these in communication in a theatrical piece.

How do you remember the experience of performing *Pool Piece* for its target audience?

It was a very therapeutic show. We went to the same schools four times, doing the show for the same kids each time. The show was slightly different each time it evolved.

We got to know the children really well. Normally when you do a children's show, you see them for an hour, and then you leave. With this show we saw the children four times, for an hour each time, over four weeks. It was just amazing to see how the relationships developed and how the kids felt freer to explore the set, the water, the actors and the musical instruments. You saw their confidence grow with each week that passed. For me, it was an amazing experience to see how theatre can work like that.

It was very interesting for me, as someone who works in music therapy, which is all about how people's relationship to music can help them to develop, feel good about themselves or learn to interact. In that sense, I thought *Pool Piece* was very therapeutic.

I had worked with Oily Cart in 1999 on the swimming pool show *Big Splash*, and I was prepared for it because I had worked with the company before. Really, Oily Cart's work is about the proximity of performer to audience member, whether that is in the water or on dry land. That proximity is an amazing thing. Of course with water you add so many different ways in which you can engage the audience. For me, performing the pool shows was a beautiful experience.

With *Pool Piece* the kids were able to have a theatrical experience that was tailored to their needs. A theatrical environment was created especially for them; that is hardly ever done for kids with learning disabilities, and especially kids with profound and multiple learning disabilities.

When these kids are at shows, they are often expected to be very passive. If you work with a child who is in a wheelchair and who has profound and multiple learning disabilities, their world is so small. Often they can't see further than 50 centimetres and because they are confined to that little area around their wheelchair, their world is very small. It's very hard for them to engage with something that's three metres away, because that's not their world. If you have an actor who holds you in the water, who helps you float, who sings for you or blows bubbles for you just five centimetres away from where you are, that proximity is so important. Oily Cart are really brilliant in opening up those worlds for those children.

With the pool shows there were many occasions on which you as a performer would feel a positive response from the children. Later, after the performance, we would also get feedback, for example from a teacher who would say of a child, 'They never usually reach out as much,' or 'They never flicker their eyes as much,' or 'They never move or wriggle in the water as much.' So even if we didn't know the child very well and couldn't really read their responses, the staff would notice different behaviours that indicated their pleasure.

Also with *Pool Piece*, we got to know the children because we performed the show for them four times. You really got to know them and you could listen out for the little sounds that people make and look out for little movements, a flickering of the eyes, a smile or just a little clench of the fist. We were looking for all those really small changes and reacting to them. In the show we did a lot of intensive interaction; you pick up on the intensity of movement or sound coming from the person you are working with and you respond to that, sometimes with a similar sort of sound or with a similar intensity. It's a bit like a mother with her baby. Water is a very maternal environment anyway, it's evocative of the womb and it's very containing, it holds you. That, I think, is one of the reasons that a lot of the kids we worked with felt very secure about being able to connect with us.

What are your favourite memories of performing with Oily Cart?

I did *Blue* [for children with complex disabilities]. We did it twice [in 2006 and 2007], so I did it for a year. I have to say, singing those songs – four shows a day, four days a week, for a year – I'm still not bored with the songs. That sums up how I feel about Oily Cart: their creativity, the music, the sets were always amazing, and the thought that was put into the shows was fantastic.

The other great thing about their work is that it's never patronising to their audience. The quality is so high, everything always looks amazing. You can just see, when the audience comes in – whether it be the children or the parents or whoever – everyone is always impressed because of the attention to detail. There was a real story attached to the props and musical instruments, they always fitted in with the narrative. Even if the story might just be that we're going on a train journey, the use of props and musical instruments made the train journey very real.

So *Blue* was a real highlight for me. Obviously I had friends who came to see it, and everyone was really impressed by the complexity but also the simplicity of the show. Similarly, the feedback from teachers would very often be about how effective the show was, even though they made it seem so simple.

Working with Oily Cart, I love the fact that as a performer you are given space to wait for a reaction from the child you are working with. If an autistic child needs to clap his hands for a few minutes, that's fine, and it can be part of the show. There is space to integrate all the various behaviours of the children. The work is both very spacious and very structured.

Sjaak van der Bent performed in

Hunky Dory! (1998); *Pass the Parcel* (1998); *Big Splash!* (1999); *The Genie's Lamp and the Ship of Gold* (2004); *King Neptune and the Pirate Queen* (2005); *Blue* (2006); *Big Balloon* (2006); *Pool Piece* (2008).

Interview with Alex Harvey
*Joint artistic director of aerial theatre company
Ockham's Razor and collaborator with Oily Cart on
Something in the Air (2009-2012)*

Please describe the process of preparation for *Something in the Air* (2009)

It started with Oily Cart just wanting to consult with us [Ockham's Razor] about how to go about creating an aerial show for people on the autistic spectrum and people with profound and multiple learning disabilities. We just got so interested in the idea that we decided that we'd really like to be performing in it.

As soon as we decided we wanted to do the piece together, we set a time and went straight into the rehearsal room. We did a lot of research and development work on the ways that we could pick people up and fly people who couldn't support their own weight. That was a really interesting time.

We had worked in the past with Amici, who are an integrated dance theatre company of disabled and non-disabled performers, but not on this sort of interactive level. Also, a lot of people in Amici are a lot more high-functioning than many of the children and young adults who were the intended audience for *Something in the Air*.

The collaboration meant that we were helping Oily Cart to discover the techniques of aerial theatre, and they were helping us to learn how to interact with children and young people on the autistic spectrum and with profound and multiple learning disabilities. In terms of us working with them on the aerial side of it, we just got loads of different chairs into the room and we rigged up different solutions and possibilities for lifting people, to see which different kinds of movement were interesting and would be pleasurable or stimulating for the audience. We tried these out on each other.

Obviously, Tim [Webb] and Claire [de Loon] have a wealth of experience in terms of which kinds of movement have been successful in the past, and a very good understanding of what sort of thing would be enjoyable or stimulating. We just had a really good time and got lots of other people in and tested their reactions to things we were experimenting with.

In terms of them teaching us how to work with that kind of audience, we would ask questions along the way, like, 'What variety of disability would this appeal to?' or, 'What sort of people would like this?' And Tim would just immediately say, 'Stop trying to label people' and, 'Stop thinking of people in that way.' He explained that the best way to work with this kind of audience is to just count everyone as an individual person who goes through the world in a slightly different way. That was very liberating and very helpful.

We went into the Michael Tippett School in Brixton [in South London] and worked with the kids who were there. We tried stuff out on them and did practice performances. That was the first time we really started to learn what it was we were going to be doing. We hadn't really realised how the show would develop until we actually started working with them. That was a very steep learning curve.

The set-up that Tim, Claire and Max [Reinhardt] had given us had prepared us for the way to approach it. Their advice was really to get in there and do it.

In terms of how our aerial theatre techniques fitted with the Oily Cart aesthetic, we showed Tim what we could do and he would say, 'Those things are interesting and those things will work.' Then we developed the characters we would play with him, and he would come in for a bit and direct us.

A lot of the time we were working with Max as well, because Tim was working with the actors who would be embedded in the school, preparing the kids for their visit to the show. So a lot of the time we were working with Max on the music side of it and co-ordinating the movement with the music.

It was a very fluid, very natural relationship. We all just were in the room together, working to develop these characters within what we were comfortable with and the way we were comfortable performing. So we'd alight upon the way we were most confident interacting and develop the characters towards that. Then Tim would advise us on what was working and what wasn't.

There were three Ockham's Razor performers in the show – myself, Charlotte Mooney and Tina Koch – and when the piece was at its biggest, I think there were as many as nine actors embedded in schools, plus the two musicians. The actors rehearsed separately from us, then joined us for the practice performances. In the show, their characters looked after the audience members and they also functioned as chair drivers, operating the movement of the chairs and making sure there was always a good link between themselves and us, ensuring that we could always see each other. There were also the songs that would happen throughout the show, which they would sing. The support that we [the Ockham's Razor performers] received from the Oily Cart performers was excellent. It was all very seamless.

How do you remember the experience of performing *Something in the Air* for its target audience?

It was immensely rewarding. It was like a baptism of fire. It was just a question of committing to it and not being embarrassed or uncomfortable. For me, it was a case of really going for it and committing at the same level as the other Oily Cart performers, who were more experienced at working with that sort of audience.

It was a wonderful experience to see a group of disabled people enter a room and, an hour later, you were saying goodbye to a group of people you had really got to know. You would really make a connection with each person in the audience. It was wonderful getting to know them as individuals, rather than just seeing them as disabled people. That happened three times a day. Our confidence grew with each performance.

Sometimes you can have the dilemma of not really knowing the extent to which you are being successful, in the sense that you can't necessarily read the responses of a child with profound and multiple learning disabilities. However, very often it's totally tangible. As with a lot of Oily Cart shows there really were a lot of audience members who had very deep reactions to the show and who had greater levels of interaction than had been seen with them before.

Working on the piece has inspired us for the work we're doing now. The next Ockham's Razor show is much more interactive and has a much closer relationship between the audience and the performers. In fact, the audience will be on the stage with us – they won't be seated in the auditorium.

What are your favourite memories of performing with Oily Cart?

The greatest moments are when you have that very special connection with some of the children. There was a wonderful little boy who is on the autistic spectrum who just narrated the entire show. It was a real joy for us. He was just so funny and brilliant. He just chatted the whole way through it and told us, with incredible imagination, what we were doing. At the end, when the chairs came down to land, he was saying, 'Oh yes, I can see the airstrip in the distance, and we're all coming in to land now. It's a very beautiful airstrip, and I can see the trees,' and so he went on. It was wonderful. We were all in fits of laughter throughout the show, and trying to hold it together. It totally changed the show, and made it a different experience.

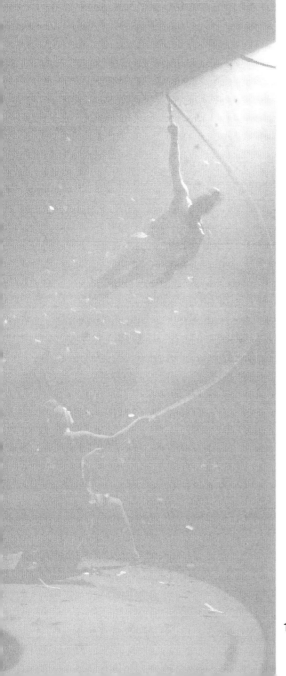

Interview with Patrick Lynch
Performer and director with Oily Cart, 2001-2005

Please describe the process of preparation for *Jumpin' Beans* (2002)

It wasn't the first show I'd done for Oily Cart. That was *Under Your Hat* (2001) and then I did a few shows for young people with special educational needs. So, I didn't need to be introduced to the Oily Cart philosophy. As usual, in rehearsals for *Jumpin' Beans* we did quite a few workshops. We went into nurseries and just hung out with the kids really, and got to know a bit more about that age group.

Before we did that, it was very hard to imagine what we might be doing in terms of performing for that age group. I don't think any of us – apart from Tim [Webb], Claire [de Loon] and Max [Reinhardt] – had a good idea what to do. I remember that after the nursery visits I began to get a sense of what you could do. I saw how one-year-olds could still be an audience. You might think that they'll be off in a world of their own but they're not really. They can all look and participate in the same sort of way.

We did workshops that were about toning down your energy levels. You don't need to be really big when you're performing to this age group. So, we were looking at how we could become small in the way that we delivered things. Those kinds of experiences were the most valuable – just getting into direct contact with that age group.

Besides that, the main elements in preparation were technical. Quite often with Oily Cart's work, if you don't have the sets, the costumes and the props [when you are rehearsing], it's actually quite difficult.

For *Jumpin' Beans* I got my puppet and started doing some of the puppeteering, and we got hold of the inflatable set. It was a little more complicated and ambitious than other work I'd done with the company, because it had three different levels to it, for three different age groups. You had to learn three different shows in a way, and be able to switch between these quite different ages.

How do you remember the experience of performing *Jumpin' Beans* for its target audience?

It was a challenge. I found in the end that it was harder doing the piece for the older age group [two to four-year-olds]; I was more comfortable performing it for the youngest [six months old]. Perhaps I found the two-year-olds more difficult because they were more boisterous. I do work now for that age group [two to four-year-olds]. Maybe it was just something I felt personally at that time.

I particularly enjoyed doing the performances for the youngest kids and was always fascinated by the fact that you could always get an audience, even of that age. The children had a shared experience of the show, and would take things from it.

We had a great time doing the show. The kids were loving it. There was a lot of interaction. The children would give us all sorts of great ideas on how to get a bird up in its nest, things like that.

Doing work for the two to four-year-old age group was always hilarious. We always had a great reception for that work. I do think, with Oily Cart, that's where their strength really lies.

When we did the *Jumpin' Beans* for the older kids [two to four years old], we had a bouncy play area and they'd have a very physical, kinetic experience there. Then they would come into the inflatable set with us [the actors] where there was a story. The story for four-year-olds was about a baby bird that had fallen out of its nest. So the kids had to get the baby bird back into its nest and make the nest comfortable.

It was a small space and we didn't have a lot of kids in there so it was a very relaxed show to perform. You could just chat with the children, and so on. It was a great show and it was very theatrical but the way the company had set it up you could try to do whatever the kids suggested. That was always the best way to do it, because they'd always come up with marvellous ideas, much more interesting than anything we [the performers] could think of. In terms of trying to get the bird into the nest – whether by making it a space rocket, building it a ladder or going up in a cloud – you can try to do all of these things.

The show was received very well by the children. With the youngest group (six months old) you got parents who were just as sceptical as anybody else; you could tell they were thinking, 'My baby's not going to get anything out of this.' I think they were won over, though. It was things as simple as flying the babies up and down all together, in time with the music. It was all very sensory.

Everything was done through the parents. We [the performers] wouldn't pick up the children, the parents would do that themselves. Or if there weren't enough parents, we would ask nursery teachers to do it. Occasionally, if we had a play group and there weren't enough parents or playgroup workers, we would ask permission to pick the babies up.

Doing everything through the parents is the best formula [when working with very young children] I think. It's the formula I use as well in my own work. It avoids lots of complications. When children first come into a show, they won't trust us [the performers] because they're just coming into this space, and they're seeing these strange people, dressed in strange costumes. So if you try to do anything with them directly, it's probably not going to work.

I think everyone [parents, nursery teachers etc] was very pleased with the production; I don't think we had anyone who said, 'This was a waste of time.' In large part, that was down to the relaxed atmosphere. The parents would come in, and they could see that we know what we're doing so they could relax too. They could just enjoy it, maybe just enjoy the time away from caring directly for the child – but even that it is worthwhile.

What are your favourite memories of performing with Oily Cart?

It's got to be working with Tim and Max, because I have the same sort of humour as them. My favourite memories are of actually making the shows, rather than doing them. Doing them, you always have a lot of heavy touring. It's really very hard work. You're travelling, setting up the show, then taking it down and moving on to the next place. In a sense, it's quite hard to enjoy that.

The best thing was being around Tim and Max because they're always ready for a joke, unless Tim got pissed off about something – and then you knew it. We still do it – they'll still call me Mother Theresa and all sorts of weird names instead of Patrick Lynch. That's what I love about Oily Cart, that irreverence they bring to their work. They're extremely serious, but they're not up their own arses. They have a sense of humour about everything. Although they're absolutely dedicated to the final project, they don't push it too hard; it's actually more of a gentle way to allow the work to emerge. They create a fun atmosphere. You can joke around and be silly. That's what it all comes down to, being silly – but silly in a serious way.

I had a good time when I was directing *If All the World Were Paper*, that was fun. It was a challenge and it was lovely to do.

Oily Cart's interactive way of working with kids is extremely scary. But the children come up with the most interesting things, as I say. They're not strictly logical and they're not trying to say the most interesting thing (if you try to say an interesting thing, it's never interesting), they just say what's in their head.

Under Your Hat was probably the scariest show I did with Oily Cart in this regard. We went into schools and had a two-day residence. We worked directly with the classes in creating stories. At the end of the two days we would have to act these stories out.

The version in theatres was even scarier. I remember I was the character of Glove. I was really scared, especially when we played the Royal Festival Hall. We had a whole rack of weird costumes, and the kids would choose costumes for each of the four of us and we'd have to improvise something in front of them. Obviously it had to be a satisfying story, with a beginning, a middle and an end. We were acting it out as we were inventing it. You do get comedy impro groups that do this, don't you? But we didn't really have very much experience of doing that and, I have to say, it quite often fell flat on its face. But the times when it did work were amazing, it was like flying without an engine, like you'd done a magic trick. It was as if you knew psychically what the other actor was about to do. It worked, but it's a risky thing that they do.

That's an extreme example. Mainly, the way Oily Cart works is to make it seem like the kids have complete freedom. But they don't. Tim's very clever in that way. You know where you want the children to go and you guide them there, but you make them feel they've made a difference. So they've invested in the show, they're part of it, and they feel closer to it, obviously.

But really, my favourite memories are just of the fun and silliness of working with Oily Cart. I'd look forward to going in every day and just seeing what we'd come up with. I just have memories of laughing all the time.

Patrick Lynch performed in

Under Your Hat (2001); *Boing!* (2002); *Jumpin' Beans* (2002); *Moving Pictures* (2003).

He also directed *If All The World Were Paper* (2005).

Interview with Lucy Angell-John
Performer with Oily Cart since 2006

Please describe the process of preparation for the babies' and toddlers' version of *Drum* (2010)

Before I joined Oily Cart I'd taught children dance classes, but I'd never worked with them in such a sensory, interactive way. When I performed in *Baby Balloon* it was only a year after I had graduated from university so my performance experience was based around contemporary dance at university; short projects with different companies, that sort of thing. Then I was working at The Place, the contemporary dance school in London, teaching children, and they told me about the audition with Oily Cart.

Since working with the company, I've gone on to do a lot more therapeutic work, with both children and mothers who have experienced violence. Oily Cart has influenced what I do quite a lot – for example, I do a lot of mother and toddler classes that are based around sensory work.

The process of creating *Drum* was very interesting because we had two weeks of research and development. We had lots of props and we spent a lot of time just playing around with things and getting a feel for what was magical for us as performers and just as human beings. We thought that what we enjoyed, babies would enjoy. It was just a question of being as creative as we could with the various props – for instance, what could we do with this bag of rice and the drum? We were given various sensory objects and asked to play around with them and think about how we could use them artistically.

Of course, the play needs a structure for the show to work. The structured aspect comes from Tim's ideas as to the different aspects that we're going to focus on. The structure comes from the themes, in this case, things like the feathers, the rice and the idea that babies like simple shapes – which gave rise to the puppets on the drum. When all those things are in place, you have a structure to work within, and Tim, as director, helps to piece it all together.

I always feel like I'm not really acting in Oily Cart pieces because it comes so naturally. Perhaps that is because it comes from a process that I have helped to develop and that sits comfortably with me. There is a lot of team work in an Oily Cart show, and it does come down to what feels right for everybody. I always feel very much a part of making the pieces.

It's fun to make a character that is in itself quite like a child. Perhaps that's another reason that it doesn't feel like acting to me, because, I think, I'm naturally quite childlike creatively. It's always come quite naturally to me to relate to children. I've always worked with children in some way or another. I seem to get on with very young children very well and they seem comfortable with me.

As ever with Oily Cart's work, design and music were crucial to creating *Drum*. Given its title, you'd expect music to be a very important part of the show. There are also lots of songs developed around the music. The show is very music led. The live music is such a big part of the Oily Cart world; it has such a high quality and such a capacity to take you to another, magical place.

As the drums are three meters wide, they're also at the centre of the design. One of the key starting points for the show was Claire's idea of using simple shapes and stripes, things that six-month-old babies will focus on. Then we started experimenting with which sounds would come out of which drum. We asked ourselves questions such as was it going to be too loud a sound for a six-month-old? Because we did really, really bash the drum and made a loud sound that vibrated across the floor.

How do you remember the experience of performing *Drum* for its target audience?

When we first started performing the show, we were all really curious to see whether babies would be shocked by the noise from the drums. In fact, hardly any babies were shocked by it; it was usually the parents who worried about their children's reactions. It was really interesting that babies were hardly ever upset by this loud, booming noise.

This experimental approach to performance is typical of Oily Cart. The work is ever evolving. If things don't work, we'll change them on tour. Sometimes things happen by accident and if they're really good, we'll adapt the show to include them.

Because it's such an intimate audience – you've only got, in the case of *Drum*, fifteen babies – there's more room for one-to-one interaction. There's no fourth wall between the performers and the audience. In Oily Cart shows for babies and toddlers, the children are free to come and sit up on the stage (which they often do), or crawl up to you and put their face next to your face and stare into your eyes for five minutes, or crawl over to the musical instruments and touch them, if that's what they're interested in. So it's in the nature of the work that you're constantly adapting.

I loved doing *Drum* because I really did feel like I was in the magical Oily Cart world while I was performing in it. It was really lovely to be able to have special moments with babies or mothers during the show. We would have play sections when we, as performers, could interact individually with each baby. Every show was different because every baby would react differently to what you were doing.

I also liked the fact that you get instant reactions from six months to two-year-olds. They're not polite about their emotions, they either come in and start crying their eyes out and want to leave (which doesn't happen very often) or they're smiling from ear to ear, really curious and blown away by it. I like the fact that you can tell straight away whether they're enjoying it or not.

What are your favourite memories of performing with Oily Cart?

Rehearsals are always lots of fun. Everyone has a laugh and enjoys themselves. Tim and Max are very funny people to work with.

I love going into rehearsals and being amazed by the new ideas they've come up with and thinking, 'How on Earth did they come up with that?' Often it seems like such a simple idea but they are just able to make it really magical.

After every show, audience members will come up to you and say something like, 'I've never seen my baby react like that, it was really amazing.' It's a really great feeling and very fulfilling. It's immediate gratification, as a performer, but you get immediate reactions, whether from babies or children with special needs. There's a connection; you can see and hear their enjoyment.

Also, with it being such an intimate performance space, children will start talking to you about things, even though you're performing. I love the fact that you never know what's going to happen. You might get a baby who just comes up and sits on you for the whole of the performance or you might have to change the show a bit because there's a baby lying in the middle of the stage.

Being an Oily Cart performer you're given the freedom and encouragement to use your own intuition during a performance. If it feels right to you and it feels right to the audience, then that's probably the right way of working. It's been very interesting for me, as a dancer who was interested in working with children through dance, to be able to add this other layer of sensory work. That in turn has fed into my interest in doing therapeutic work.

Another great thing about Oily Cart's work is the world that it creates. You can't make that up with children, I think they see through it. It really has to be magical and beautiful – I don't think the children would buy into it if it wasn't. That's especially true of young children, who really take things at face value. For example, performers' facial expressions; because young children read them so clearly, they have to be honest and natural.

It also has to feel magical and beautiful to the parents because babies are reading their parents' reactions constantly. That's why the company's shows work so well: it's so high quality and so magical that it engages adults as much as it does children.

When you perform in or see an Oily Cart show it just makes sense that theatre for children should be like this. You think, 'It's so beautiful, why isn't more children's theatre like this?' It's not at all patronising either, that's what I like about it. It's got really good, high quality music and design, which makes you feel really good as a performer. I feel very privileged to have worked with them.

Lucy Angell-John performed in

Baby Balloon (2006-08); *Drum* (2010-12).

Interview with Geoff Bowyer
Performer with Oily Cart, 1987-1997

Please describe the process of preparation for *A Peck of Pickled Pepper* (1994)

The show was about making a cake and about the ingredients that would go into it. We had a four-week rehearsal period as we did for all the shows, whether it was work for young children or shows for kids with special educational needs. Tim would write the script (during his holidays usually) and we'd get that at the beginning of the rehearsal period. From there we would develop the performance, all of Max's music and Claire's wonderful costumes.

With Oily Cart's work, there is a script but within it you're also expected to fly by the seat of your trousers. We know the sorts of questions that we are going to be asking the children, like, 'What ingredients go into a cake?' and 'Where does milk come from?' And then a puppet cow comes round on a turntable and it's milked in front of the children by the farmer. So because of the level of interactivity between the performers and the children, the actors have to be actors of a certain kind.

You will be taken off the script but you have to stick to where you are in the story because some little child will say, 'Milk doesn't come from a cow, it comes from a bottle.' Then the comedy will arise, and Tim will know that when he writes the script. In fact even if a child doesn't intervene, Tim might have done it in advance in rehearsal, saying something like, 'Eh Geoff, hold on a minute! It comes from a milk bottle, doesn't it?' We have to work like that, and with special needs children in particular it is dynamite.

How do you remember the experience of performing *A Peck of Pickled Pepper* for its target audience?

It was great to be wrestling with a problem that was written to go wrong, so the kids can solve it. And the kids would laugh at us and they'd get up and solve the theatrical problem set by Tim's writing.

As with all Oily Cart shows, there was this wonderful shift in emphasis. Although we were adults working with children, we weren't authority figures. We didn't know more than the children. In fact we knew less than they did. We needed their help. The children would think, 'Look at that silly man up there. Why is he trying to put a label on a packet of a dozen eggs with a six inch nail and a hammer?'

In the show we had a great big turntable on which were all the ingredients and the entire story of how to make a cake, with details like visiting a bee-hive to get the honey. All the objects needed for making the cake would come round on the turntable, with [the actor] Jonny Quick sitting in the middle looking just like the man in the bowler hat in the Magritte paintings.

The characters – such as the chef and the famer – would have a series of problems. The chef would say, 'oh dear! I've got to make a cake, but I don't know what to put in it.' This would become a massive problem for thousands of children all over England.

What are your favourite memories of performing with Oily Cart?

There are simply too many to choose from, but I always loved developing a character. My character, George Broadbent, was a horrible man [George Broadbent was the central character in a series of shows for children with severe learning disabilities, which Oily Cart did between 1993 and 1996, and in which the company spent two days in a given school. The shows included *Georgie Goes to Hollywood* and *George After a Fashion*]. I used to have so much fun with things going wrong for him. The kids always had to save him. It's wonderful when you know you're doing it well by getting it badly wrong. The most enduring memory is of seeing the kids satisfied that they'd done it, that they'd solved the problem. I can't top that.

The special needs shows also gave me some of the greatest experiences I ever had, because you were taken well off your script then. The show would still need to have a structure and we would have to get out of it. You cannot be prepared in advance for every question that children might ask, especially in Special Needs schools. For example, a kid could say to me out of the blue, 'That's not a donkey, and don't forget to take the chef's keys back.' Now, that makes absolutely no sense to me, but returning the chef's keys might have been that child's job in the school. That sort of thing can come at you so quickly and you have to handle it and incorporate it into the show. There's nobody quite like Oily Cart in preparing actors for that kind of interaction.

We would have these songs in which we put each child's name into the verse. The staff of the Special Needs schools would always tell us how much the children enjoyed that. Often there were children with such severe physical disabilities that their response wasn't always clear to us from their facial expressions. But the staff, who knew the children well, would say things like, 'She's really enjoying it, you can tell by the way her eyelids are fluttering a lot.' That was very rewarding.

Likewise, the shows for children aged four to six years old. The kids would willingly suspend their disbelief and go with the flow of the show. There would be points when they would be asked to get involved. It's not like in pantomime – 'Where's the ghost?', 'He's behind you!'- it's not that. Rather, there are points in Oily Cart shows where the children become central; there may be a song to sing or there'd be situations with costumes that involve the children. In Special Needs shows this sort of thing was nearly non-stop. You had to be on your toes.

The qualities you have to have to be able to learn how to do that are beyond acting. These are the sorts of things that actors would normally not like to do because you are doing this directly for the kids, you're solving a problem with them, for them. That is a skill in itself, and hanging onto your character while you do it is most important for the entire range of our precious young audiences.

I always felt privileged to be working with such actors and earning a living in a very good administration. Oily Cart were always very good on the administrative side, things like making sure all hotels were booked. When you arrived in town, you knew exactly where you were going. We knew we were all staying in the same hotel and that we had our own rooms. These things are important and Oily Cart always did them very well.

Tim and Oily Cart have been most fortunate in the actors they have had because most of them get it. They get what it means to go the extra twenty miles for the young audience. People like Jonny Quick, Carol Walton, Paulette Brown, Sue Eves and Nicky McRae – there were many others, of course. All of us actors would go beyond the call of duty because we knew what we were letting ourselves in for.

Whenever Tim held auditions for a special needs show, he would be very thorough because the company's reputation in this area was growing all the time. He needed the continuity. The same continuity he'd had with his founder members, namely Claire, Max and himself.

That's what sets Oily Cart apart: first and foremost, the way Tim thinks. It's how he thinks it, how Claire visualises it and how Max hears it.

I'm proud that Oily Cart was my life for ten years. The magic that came from those three people – Tim, Max and Claire – the magic of the writing, the music and the design will always put Oily Cart in a class of its own for me. The world they create is for our most precious audiences – children and children and young adults with special needs.

Geoff Bowyer performed in

Bermuda Rectangle (1987); *Playhouse* (1988); *Pleasuredome* (1989); *Chest of Drawers* (1989); *Colour Me Colour You* (1990); *Red Lorry Yellow Lorry* (1990); *Will it Hurt?* (1990); *Funky Philharmonic* (1991); *Off the Wall* (1991); *Dinner Ladies From Outer Space* (1992); *Greenfingers* (1992); *EuroBroadbent* (1993); *A Bit Missing* (1993); *Georgie Goes To Hollywood* (1994); *A Peck of Pickled Pepper* (1994 & 1998); *George After a Fashion* (1995); *Perfect Present* (1995); *Tickled Pink* (1996); *George Sells Out* (1996); *Roly Poly Pudding* (1996); *Over the Moon* (1997).

Interview with Nicole Worrica
Performer with Oily Cart since 1999

Please describe the process of preparation for Play House (1999)

The preparation started during my audition, the second part of which was to engage with young kids from the school next door [Smallwood Primary School, South London, where Oily Cart is based]. Tim wasn't just looking for performers who could learn lines and do a performance; he wanted to know how good we were at interacting with kids. I remember doing a poem by Benjamin Zephaniah. Knowing that it had to be interactive, I kind of co-created the poem with the young kids. I got them involved and followed their lead.

I was given the job [performing in *Play House*]. My character was called Fluff and my sense was touch. We were a team of four girls and we were all builders and we played brass instruments.

We started off by going into nurseries. We played our brass instruments and were singing about how we were these builders, and how we were coming into their nursery and we'd be staying here for a couple of days, and was that alright by them? So we started off by asking their permission. They'd say 'yes', and we'd install ourselves with our big orange crates that had lots of craft materials and sensory materials inside. We used these materials to make things with the kids, which in turn informed the show we were going to create at the end of the two days.

We then toured the show and we ended up at the Half Moon Young People's Theatre [in East London]. When we were there, we created an even more theatrical set, and the show was based upon the work that we'd done in the schools, which was all about the different senses. So in addition to me as Fluff (touch), there was Zoot (who was into sound), Dazzle (for whom everything was visual) and there was Sniff (who liked to smell).

115

How do you remember the experience of performing *Play House* for its target audience?

It was a real lesson for me. I was probably attracted to Oily Cart in the first place because of the big kid in myself and my own love of play, and I also loved the simplicity of the work.

[In *Play House*] I liked being this big character, who was much bigger than the kids; I called the children 'my little friends'. I played a Columbo detective-like character who was very curious about what the kids had to offer. I was very interested in where they would take me – rather than saying, 'Right, we're going to do this today.' I also really enjoyed playing the fool a little bit and that seemed to work for the children. They were the important ones, they were the ones who knew what to do, and I was the one who followed along, in a bit of a bumbling manner, quite curious and wide-eyed. That was nice for that age group just to have this big person who isn't an authority figure, a big person who's less important than them. That was a nice experience.

I remember when we would initially come in as strangers, four women blasting out these loud noises – particularly with me playing the trumpet, which was awful – you would see a slight scaredness on the part of the kids about these strangers in bright clothes coming in. Yet by the end of the two days there was a sadness, because the children had got attached to us so quickly and they'd so quickly got over the fact that there were four scary people coming into their nursery or school. They'd become totally engaged in that world of fantasy figures. The turnaround was so quick.

It was also interesting that the kids who the teachers least expected to became very attached to us very quickly, the kids who they never expected to do anything, and who they never pushed forward for anything – those kids really came out of their shells. Discovering that stood me in good stead for my later work.

I also learned that performing for kids didn't have to be high energy all the time. You could just sit alongside quietly while a child was drawing away, or doing a craft activity.

Mainly, though, it was about play and the chance to be silly. It was so simple. I hardly spoke; it was really a non-verbal process and when it's non-verbal, it's richer.

What are your favourite memories of performing with Oily Cart?

The thing that has surprised me most, out of all the shows I've done with the company, and that is really lovely and always continues to surprise me is the response you get when you're doing work for people with special educational needs, and you allow them to do the leading. You always get a better story. If, as a performer, you just sit and wait, it's always surprising what comes out the other end. You're not being intrusive with the person at all; you really are just sitting, waiting, hanging on and putting your trust in them that they're going to come out with something. It might be something they say while you're performing; you're always keeping an ear out for what they're saying so that you can respond to it, rather than just going on and on with your lines. I think that is the beauty of Oily Cart.

There are boundaries but you always allow yourself to come off script and then you go back again, you're coming in and out, it's like breathing. That makes for a much richer show, because it's like a co-created performance between you and the person you're performing for.

This way of working comes from Tim [Webb] and Max [Reinhardt]. When you're with them you always get the sense that they have never changed their ethics throughout the lifetime of the company. If anything, they've pared it down even more, made it even more simple, giving even more time for the young person to respond. They've just got this knack – they're playful characters themselves, which makes them really good to be around.

They almost model for their performers how they want us to be. So for instance, they bring out and encourage my love of playing around with sounds or movements. They'll let me play with it over and over, to create my own character. It's within directorial boundaries of course but they will allow that freedom of silliness and play, and what comes out of play. Then we start forming the production. Out of a kind of chaos, we end up with a structure.

In terms of specific experiences, I loved doing *Pool Piece* (2008). You were in a swimming pool for 45 minutes. You'd splash the water and let the sound hang, and wait for one of the young people to respond, then you'd respond to them. There's something special about that; it's just total, non-verbal tuning in.

But my favourite experience ever, in any job I've ever done, came from doing a piece for children with autism and special educational needs. We were doing a show called *Blue* (2006). [There were two sides to *Blue*. For the most part, it was a 55-minute long touring production going into Special Needs schools and theatre venues. But for the 2007 Manchester International Festival Oily Cart embedded additional characters for one week in two of the Special Needs schools who were to visit the touring production playing in the G-Mex Conference Centre. Nicole Worrica was one of them.]

117

I wanted to look at what it was like for the young people to meet one of the characters before the performance. I wanted to know if they would interact more when they saw the show. So I went into a school in Manchester for two weeks. These were kids on the autistic spectrum. We built a shack in the yard of their school. I had my bed in there, an old record player, lots of boxes of sensory stuff for activities. The kids believed I lived in this shack but I was going home every night and coming in really early.

I just embedded myself in that school and I didn't want to leave. I had the most amazing time. I remember this one guy, he was massive. He must have been about sixteen years old. As the teachers said, he wasn't ready to join the sessions I held in the back yard – he was a bit frightened. He'd gone into a lot of hyper-arousal and he seemed really tense. So I went with a teacher, and followed this young man into the sensory room. I started to sing and I went down gently on the floor with him, and I remember he took off his socks and stuck his feet out to be massaged. It was so fantastic to achieve that response through creativity. With autism you're so hyper-sensitive to sound and light and you get distressed very quickly. It was a really lovely moment.

Being in that school was very successful. When the kids came to see the show, I'd already shown them pictures of all the characters and given them descriptions of each of them. So when they met the characters it was like I was handing it over. They were so excited to see all these characters that they knew, because we'd been talking about them and living and breathing them for two weeks. I didn't want to leave that school.

People say ridiculous things like, 'If you're autistic, you don't have empathy,' which is utter rubbish. I remember this young guy at the school in Manchester. As I was leaving after being there for two weeks, he looked at me and he looked really sad; he said, 'Who am I going to play my computer with now?' We just looked at each other. That was just his way of saying, 'I'm going to miss you'. It was just so lovely. I thought, 'Oh no, I'm going to cry!' And the teacher was really crying, because he was blown away by just how much they'd engaged with the piece over the two weeks. It was really brilliant. I don't think I'll ever top that for a job.

Nicole Worrica performed in

Play House (1999); *Dreams and Secrets* (2000); *Knock! Knock! Who's There* (2000); *The Genie's Lamp and the Ship of Gold* (2004); *King Neptune and the Pirate Queen* (2005); *If All the World Were Paper* (2007); *Pool Piece* (2008).

Perspectives on Oily Cart

More than most theatre companies, Oily Cart's work is of interest to a wide and diverse array of people, from young children and children and young people with learning disabilities; to the relatives, teachers and carers of those children; through to theatre makers; academic researchers; and theatre critics. This section of the book is a selection of analyses, comments and reviews across the full range of Oily Cart's oeuvre.

Drum 2010

The Free Spirits of Children's Theatre
Tony Graham

'If the theatre had been built for just this show, it would have been worth it,' said Joanna Kennedy, the Chair of the Unicorn Theatre [in London], on seeing *Something in the Air*. Oily Cart's work can move people: up in the air, around a table, under the earth and along a mole-hole. But, above all, the shows move us to laugh and cry and feel something. What I love most about Oily Cart is its chutzpah. In 2006, I was asked to speak at Oily Cart's 25th anniversary. I talked about the great sense of fun that spills out of the free-wheeling anarchy and mayhem embedded in every show. Oily Cart are the free spirits of the children's theatre movement.

I first met Tim [Webb] and Claire [de Loon] shortly after becoming artistic director of the Unicorn in 1997. The Unicorn was having one of its perennial financial crises and it looked likely that we would have to close. The company was based at The Arts Theatre near Leicester Square. It takes a crisis to discover who your friends are. Once Tim heard about our plight, he was one of the few who took up our case. These things stay with you.

I had heard of Oily Cart but didn't know them well. When I returned to London from Scotland, I went to see their work at Battersea Arts Centre. Their reputation was rising. When I thanked Tim for his support, his reply was revealing. He talked about the importance of creating a building dedicated to theatre for children. And he talked about the significance of a company that had fought for something bigger than itself. Pioneers like Caryl Jenner fought for the idea of theatre for children at a time when few acknowledged its necessity, and Tim understood this. Not mired in self-absorption, he had a wisdom and insight that transcended his own circumstance. Tim's ability to see beyond the here and now, his vision and purpose and his natural generosity – all of this is manifested in the work of the company.

Oily Cart has its roots in the liberation movements of the 60s. It's not that the company is overtly political. Rather, it shares joie de vivre, social commitment and a dramatic language that springs out of popular radical theatre. Those great companies of the 60s and 70s that brought a rough charm, a direct address to the audience, a shared attitude, an openness and disdain for authority – all that is visible in the work of the Oilies.

As the relationship between the Unicorn and Oily Cart grew, I discovered that we had more in common than a shared philosophy. Like myself, Tim and Claire had served their apprenticeship at the Citizens Theatre, Glasgow. Under the artistic leadership of Giles Havergal, Philip Prowse and Robert David MacDonald (1969- 2003), the Citizens occupied a unique place in the world of theatre. With a brilliant design aesthetic, a taste for high European and American classics, and an exquisite sense of dramaturgy and direction, the Citizens eschewed provincialism and small-mindedness. It also took spectacular risks with programming and staging while managing its books with precision. The inspiration for its sheer cheek, bravado and high classicism came from a scholarly and irreverent devotion to the world's great playwrights and artists. A deep commitment to its audiences was born at a time when radical change was in the air.

The early-seventies at the Citizens was one of the great moments in British theatre. And, great though it was, I'm not referring to Tim and Claire's first meeting there. At various times after the war, Joan Littlewood, Peter Brook and the Citizens shook British theatre to its core and redefined the rules of engagement. The very idea of an ensemble, such a European notion, was critical to all of these great theatre pioneers. And to trace the history of Oily Cart is to see the emergence of a group of artists that grew, snowball-fashion, into something bigger than the sum of its parts. Is it any wonder that Philip Prowse recognised in Claire a kindred spirit?

Prowse was the designer/director at the Citizens who defined its look, feel and shape. At the most recent Oily Cart show, *Ring a Ding Ding*, the black, white, red and gold colour scheme was redolent of the Prowsian palette. Claire de Loon's extraordinary work is profoundly under-appreciated. Were she working in another branch of theatre, I'm sure she would be hailed as one of the finest designers around. Shame on the critics and taste-mongers whose prejudices about art for children prevent them from recognising great talent. And full credit to Claire for being true to her art, for continuing to dazzle us with her witty, inspirational worlds in which audiences and performers alike share a sense of wonder and surprise.

What makes companies great? I think it has something to do with having the right blend and balance of artists. In the case of the Citizens, one can see how the direction and management of Havergal, the design aesthetic of Prowse and the literary knowledge of MacDonald was a perfect mix. If we look at the Oilies, we can see a similar picture: Tim is the consummate manager, director and frontman, Claire's design anchors the company and gives it a distinctive brand, and finally Max Reinhardt's musical taste is both playfully idiosyncratic and ambitiously exotic. This triumvirate of talents collectively creates something bigger than all of them as individuals. Many artists, performers, craftspeople, musicians and puppeteers have been connected to the company over the years but at the core is this rich creative leadership.

A number of things struck me about *Something in the Air*, a remarkable show by any standards. It was created for an audience of six young people with complex disabilities and/or an autistic spectrum disorder plus six of their helpers. It was one of the most inventive and audacious shows we had presented at the Unicorn. The scale alone was impressive. Commissioned by the Manchester International Festival, it needed a large, technically well-equipped playing space. Its lush, atmospheric, green and misty world immersed and hypnotised us from the get-go. The collaboration with the aerial theatre company Ockham's Razor led to performers lurking up in the grid, creating a mysterious presence from above; circus artistry amid the foliage. The audience was raised and lowered gently on specially designed chairs attached to the grid. And to lead us deeper into this strange, playful world, Max Reinhardt's jazz-tinged score played about us with warmth and intensity. In all of Oily Cart's shows, live music plays a fundamental role. Song and singing. Call and response. From folk to blues to jazz to sounds that defy easy classification. The instruments can be as original as the shows. Sometimes they are specially created for the production.

When I saw *Something in the Air,* I was delighted to hear the exquisite clarinet of Arun Ghosh, one of the hottest young jazz composers and improvisers playing in the UK. By chance, one of the show's musicians needed subbing that day. In place of the regular musician, I could hardly believe my ears as the soulful trumpet of Byron Wallen soared and blended into this magical world. Wallen, from a remarkable musical family, is one of the UK's classiest jazz trumpet players. Arun Ghosh and Byron Wallen played together in a show designed, on account of their needs, for no more than six participants. This kind of musical chemistry is, frankly, exceptional. I can think of few other theatre companies, let alone one in the field of theatre for young audiences, which take their music so seriously. Yet the music supports the production, never drawing attention to itself. There is a humility amongst these awesome musicians that makes their work for Oily Cart truly great.

Blue, another show accessible to those with multiple disabilities, took its name and inspiration from the world of the blues. This imaginative mixing of genres, together with placing audiences of all abilities on the same level, is what characterises the Oily philosophy. Rather than timidly following audience expectation it challenges us to share and enjoy the thrill of the un-expected. *Baby Balloon* was where I first encountered the music of Tunde Jegede. An Oily regular, Jegede is a pioneer of African classical music in the UK. He plays the cello and the kora with equal virtuosity. He is as much at home with the Brodsky Quartet as he is playing alongside the greatest African musicians.

Binding together these diverse, brilliant, improvisational world and jazz musicians is the dynamic input of Max Reinhardt, Oily Cart's third creative director along with Tim and Claire. Max's musical taste can be heard regularly on *Late Junction*, a Radio Three programme dedicated to world and contem-porary music. *Late Junction* is as difficult to define as the Oily Cart shows themselves. But what stands out is the attention to musical excellence, com-plexity and a sense of adventure.

Oily Cart's theatre is a colourful journey that involves singing, playing, story-telling, participating and sharing experience – many Oily shows involve the audience joining the actors in donning playful and witty costumes. The com-pany places the audience at the centre of the experience. Theatre for the very young and for young audiences with profound and multiple disabilities places Oily Cart in the vanguard of theatre for young audiences.

Internationally, the work of the company is highly respected and admired. This is not a sentimental response. Much work produced for early years and disadvantaged audiences is uninspiring. But the searching nature of Oily Cart's work and the complex needs of its audiences have always resulted in new and often exhilarating solutions. If Oily Cart is ahead of its peers, it's be-cause of the way the work connects with the audience. Magically, Oily Cart grows older and younger at the same time.

The Oilies' deep respect for their audience is carried over into every detail of their live performances. But it is a respect leavened by irreverence and a refusal to patronise the audience in any way. Its emphasis on producing work for audiences in their early years or with a wide spectrum of disability is somehow less significant than its quest to communicate with all of us. Carers, parents, teachers and children alike can enjoy the experience for what it is rather than because of some other agenda. It's a deeply humanising experience.

This is why Joanna Kennedy was right when she said that *Something in the Air*, a show for the very few, was a reason for us all to rejoice. The Unicorn worked hard to persuade funders and donors to build a spectacular new theatre for the young. Here was reason enough.

Tony Graham *is a freelance theatre director. He was artistic director of London's Unicorn Theatre for fourteen years (opening its new flagship theatre in 2005) and, prior to that, was artistic director of TAG Theatre, Glasgow. In 2011, he was made an Honorary Fellow of Rose Bruford Drama College.*

Oily Cart: unravelling the magic
Katherine Runswick-Cole and Dan Goodley

We first became aware of the work of Oily Cart when we were approached by Tim Webb and asked to evaluate Oily Cart's residences in schools and the performances of *Something in the Air* (2009). The production was the culmination of collaboration between Oily Cart, Ockham's Razor[1] and the Manchester International Festival, 2009.[2] The evaluation of *Something in the Air* was carried out under the umbrella of a research project that was ongoing at the time.[3] The project's aim was to explore the lives of disabled children in the 2000s and to consider how disabled children had fared under the *Every Child Matters* (DfES, 2004) policy agenda for children.

Oily Cart's work in schools and in enabling disabled children to access the arts cut across the project's areas of interest. The evaluation was an opportunity to explore the impact of the *Every Child Matters* agenda by opening up a dialogue between arts and education, facilitating an exploration of disabled children's experiences in the contemporary policy context.[4]

Undoubtedly, the full power of a production comes from witnessing it firsthand so the challenge for our evaluation of *Something in the Air* was to offer glimpses into the experiences of the production through the medium of the written word. As one father said after watching his son taking part, *Something in the Air* created a 'little bit of a miracle'. This posed a problem for us as a research team, unused to writing about miracles and sadly more used to writing about structural forms of violence and discrimination against disabled children.[5] We also feared that in evaluating the production, we might at the same time unravel the magic.

So we were treading carefully, wanting to represent the 'little bit of a miracle' that occurred in the production while at the same time recognising the difficulties of representing those experiences. Nonetheless, we recognised that finding ways of talking about the value of Oily Cart's work was crucial for disabled children, not least because disabled children have often been excluded from opportunities to participate in the arts.

Unfortunately, disabled children's participation in drama has often been focused on the therapeutic aspects of performance; for example, arts as a medium for intervention and rehabilitation in the form of dramatherapy.[6] Yet it is widely recognised that drama represents a valuable means by which children can participate in cultural activities. What is unusual and distinctive about Oily Cart is that it was the production team's aim to work with children who have traditionally been considered 'hard to reach' within education and in the arts, including children with the labels 'profound and multiple learning difficulties' and 'severe autistic spectrum disorder'. The significance of this aim was not lost on a teacher in one of the participating schools, who commented that it was good that the production was aimed at 'our hardest to reach children', as it was unusual for them to be seen as the target group.

The residencies and productions were carefully planned to engage children and young people using multisensory and interactive approaches.

Something in the Air: the performance

The performance was the culmination of the collaborative workshops held in three schools in the three weeks before the production at the Contact Theatre, in Manchester in July, 2009.[7] There was no formal script for the performance but the following summary[8] outlines what happens at the performances:

- The audience arrived outside the venue and followed a trail (eg of red leaves) that led to the performance space. In a separate room, there was a Rest Nest where people could wait for their session to begin.

- In the Rest Nest the audience were fitted with their seat belts, and decisions were made about what kind of chair was needed: upright, lying back or wheelchair platform.

- Each of the young participants brought with them something wonderful – and red – that they hoped would attract the Nest People down and help them to make friends with them. They had been told that they were invited to a very special Nest People party.

- As the musicians played, the characters led the six young people and their companions into the performance space where for the first time they saw the glittering flying rig and, up high, completely swathed in the green silks, the outlines of the other Nest People.

- The young people and their companions called the three Nest People down from their perches. First Sprout, then Moss and finally Pod joined the new arrivals on the floor. The family members were joyfully reunited and then the guests were introduced. Then it was time for the party to begin. Music. All danced to the seats.

- The participants were helped into their seats. Each pair of seats had at least one person, the chair driver, concentrating on each pair of participants ('D'you want to swing more?'/'D'you need to come down?').

- The chairs were hoisted into the air. The Nest People – Moss, Sprout and Pod – flew alongside and above and below the participants on the silks.

- All attention was drawn to Bramble (the rigger) as he made his tumultuous, precarious way on lines through the air from one of the legs to the centre of the rig, where he would remain for much of the subsequent action.

- Red leaves fell from high in the rig. Moss, helped by Pod, swung amongst the falling leaves on the trapeze. All seats joined in with a sympathetic swinging motion. As Moss slowed, so did the seats, until she was sitting quite still on the trapeze. She transferred onto Pod's shoulders. He carried her away from the trapeze and she was handed a large red fan. She circled the audience, fanning them. The chair drivers joined in the fanning, using smaller fans to cool the two participants in their pair of chairs.

- A small red ball was dropped from the rig by Sprout. It was allowed to bounce until there was no more movement. Then Willow, the stage manager, picked up the ball. She, Pod and Moss danced and bounced the ball around the circle formed by the audience. The chair drivers bounced the chairs in sympathetic movement.

- A medium-sized red ball was dropped by Sprout. Moss picked up the ball when it finally became still. Then she, Willow and Pod danced and bounced the balls around the circle. The chair drivers bounced the chairs in sympathetic movement.

- A very large red ball was dropped by Sprout. Pod picked up the ball when it finally became still. Then he, Moss and Willow danced and bounced the balls around the circle. The chair drivers bounced the chairs in sympathetic movement.

- Pod launched herself from the top of the rig on a bungee. She bounced like one of the balls. Then Moss and Willow began to play with her, first catapulting her from one side of the circle to another, and then throwing the big red ball to her in a game of Pig in the Middle. When Pod managed to catch the ball she was whirled round and round and round again by the force of it.

- Then shiny paper sycamore-seed shapes spiralled down from the top of the rig, glittering in the side lighting.

- Pod appeared hanging upside down from the top centre of the rig. He was wearing a costume of glittering silver. He tried, mostly in vain, to catch the sycamore shapes as they twirled past him. As he spun, his costume sparkled. Silver paper squares were scattered as he spun. The chairs danced in rhythm with his movements.

- Several slowly rotating mirrors were lowered from the rig, caught in the beams of a few sharply focused spotlights they flashed like searchlights in an otherwise intense blackout. Three of these mirrors were detached from their lines, taken round by Pod, Sprout and Moss and then used to show each of the participants his or her reflection as they were sung the Name Songs. These Name Songs, which use melodies already introduced, were sung to each participant in turn and with his or her name as the only lyric.

- A musician announced that it is now time for the visitors to get ready to go back to school or home. The School Nest People said their good-byes and gave many thanks to their friends for making such a wonderful party.

- A musician sang a goodbye song and thanked each of the children/young people for being part of the performance, as the seats were lowered to the ground and the visitors disembarked and led back into the Rest Nest area.

The magic: children and young people's responses

What follows are glimpses into the children and young people's experience of the performance):[9]

Asad was sitting in the chair at the performance, looking worried as the performers started to raise the seat into the air. A performer, familiar to Asad from school, and his teaching assistant both offered reassurance as he placed his feet firmly on the ground. As he watched the aerialists above him, one of the aerialists reached down to him and he touched her hand. ... Asad was gradually raised into the air ... By the end of the performance, Asad was smiling and laughing in the chair, enjoying the action ... (*Researcher's notes*)

At the start of the performance, Harry was wearing ear defenders. He was sitting in the chair looking relaxed but clearly didn't want to listen to the music ... a little later I noticed the ear defenders had come off, now Harry had a finger in one ear, but the other ear was uncovered ... towards the end of the performance Harry's finger was out of his ear. ... (*Researcher's notes*)

Farhan has been really motivated and engaged with activities, which is quite rare for him. He rarely chooses to have music. When he saw the nest people singing and dancing he joined in by moving to the music. (*Teacher*)

Did you see Nelam? She was tracking the helicopter spinny things. She never looks at anything. And she didn't hit herself once during the whole performance. (*Teacher*)

Greg, you're flying, you're flying higher than me ... (*Child 1*)

This is the best day of my life! (*Child 2*)

It is better than being in a spitfire! (*Child 3*)

I'm a good boy! (*Child 4*)

The children's involvement in performance challenges those who work with disabled children to recognise diverse ways of being and diverse ways of enjoying the arts. The moments captured here, though seemingly small, represent for those children what Woods (1993) has described as 'critical events in education': moments where children experience significant changes. It is through participation in an Oily Cart production that those moments are made possible.

And finally...

Investment in the arts has a unique potential to celebrate disabled children. Sadly, disabled children and young people often experience isolation and discrimination in their communities,[10] but Oily Cart offers a much needed space for disabled children and young people to be publicly recognised for their participation in and contribution to the arts, and, of course, for a little bit of magic to occur.

Katherine Runswick-Cole is Research Fellow in Disability Studies and Psychology at Manchester Metropolitan University.

Dan Goodley *is Professor of Psychology and Disability Studies at Manchester Metropolitan University. Katherine and Dan share a passion for research that challenges negative images, and celebrates the lives, of disabled children.*

Notes

1 Ockham's Razor are an aerial theatre company that combine circus and visual theatre. They perform in theatres and circuses nationally and internationally (www.ockhamsrazor.co.uk).

2 Manchester International Festival (MIF) (see: http://www.mif.co.uk/) is a festival of original work and special events that takes place in Manchester, UK, biennially. The Festival presents a wide-ranging programme designed to be 'exhilarating, thought-provoking and welcoming to all' (MIF, 2009).

3 The project was entitled *Does every child matter, post-Blair?: The interconnections of disabled childhoods*, and was funded by the Economic and Social Research Council, September, 2008 – May, 2011. It was based in the Research Institute for Health and Social Change at Manchester Metropolitan University (Visit: http://post-blair.posterous.com/ for more information).

4 Goodley and Runswick-Cole, 2011a.

5 Goodley and Runswick Cole, 2011b.

6 eg. Chesner, 1995.

7 For details see: Runswick-Cole and Goodley, 2009.

8 Adapted from Runswick-Cole and Goodley, 2009: pp.13-16.

9 Adapted from Runswick-Cole and Goodley, 2009

10 Goodley and Runswick-Cole, 2011b

References

Department for Education and Science (2004) *Every Child Matters: change for children*, London: HMSO

Chesner, A. (1995) *Drama Therapy for People with Learning Difficulties.* London: Jessica Kingsley.

Goodley, D. and Runswick-Cole, K. (2011a) Problematising policy: conceptions of 'child', 'disabled' and 'parents' in social policy in England, *International Journal of Inclusive Education* 15 (1): p71-85.

Goodley, D. and Runswick-Cole, K. (2011b) The violence of disablism, *Journal of Sociology of Health and Illness*, 33(4): p602-17.

Runswick-Cole, K. and Goodley, D. (2009) *'Better than a spitfire ride!' – an evaluation of Something in the Air? Oily Cart's Special Needs school residencies and production for Manchester International Festival, July 2009.* Available online at: www.rihsc.mmu.ac.uk/postblairproject/.

Woods, P. (1993) Critical events in education. *British Journal of Sociology of Education* 14, no. 4: p355-368.

Review

This review of *Soapsuds* by Ann McFerran appeared in *Time Out* on July 16, 1986.

A fly wearing specs, a goldfish who grows into a whale, a frog and the magical Mr Bubbleman all star in Oily Cart's latest spectacular – a sort of washday 'soap' which, on a particularly hot day recently, enraptured both children and staff of a local day nursery and had my own three year-old murmuring wistfully for Mr Bubbleman for days to come.

Our soapy saga begins when Mr Herbert Sherbert in his pink spotted under-pants decides to buy a washing machine from Miss Myrtle Turtle, so he can wash his dirty trousers. But you don't have to follow the story to enjoy this ingenious new show which brilliantly combines puppetry, songs with movement (everyone comes out humming 'plug in the plug') and some very funny comic slapstick. A first-rate, popular show for little kids.

Review

This review of *Jumpin' Beans* by Kate Stratton appeared in *Time Out* on March 12, 2003.

What do you do when you enter a theatre? Take off your coat and find your seat. But with Oily Cart it's different. Their new show for the very young is divided into three distinct experiences – for babies and toddlers from six months, for two to four-year-olds and for the four to sixes. Each audience is invited to explore a 'wibbly wobbly world of wonder' – an enticing expanse of tunnels, ball pools and shimmery mirrors – before entering giant, inflatable tent for storytime.

Play and its importance in life and art is at the heart of this intimate, low-key production, which celebrates the transforming power of the imagination. Too much theatre for adults won't admit that 'let's pretend' is at the core of every drama, but Oily Cart never suffers this hang-up. Here the performers look their audience in the eye and ask them to join in, sometimes musically, often verbally, always engagingly.

Take the finest moments in these 30-minute miniatures. For babies there's a chance to cuddle dolls and be tickled by feathers. Two to four-year-olds get to build a nest for a fluffy bird; four to six-year-olds are invited to construct a mate for Marilyn the monster. With a few plastic flowers and the twist of a feather duster, the performers lay down the rules for the kind of fantasy world in which children need no schooling. Let's pretend? Let's pretend all theatre was this much fun.

Review

This review of *Conference of the Birds* by **Mark Brown** appeared in the *Sunday Herald* on **July 5, 2005.**

Every once in a while one discovers a theatre show so special, so beautifully crafted and so emotionally affecting that one feels simply privileged to have experienced it. Conference of the Birds, by London-based children's theatre group Oily Cart, is such a production.

The company has had much critical acclaim for the professionalism and passion with which it fulfils what it describes as the 'strategic need' to produce work for the under-fours and children and young people with severe learning disabilities. Just five minutes inside the wonderful nest set of *Conference of the Birds* – a multisensory performance for youngsters with profound and multiple learning disabilities – and one is converted to the ranks of the company's admirers.

An intimate show for six children or teenagers and their carers, it is a crystal-clear, exquisitely subtle piece of theatre. Elegiac, Persian-influenced live music, light, image and performance combine with an elemental approach to the senses which has a movingly positive effect on its young audience.

As the brightly coloured birds – played with extraordinary sensitivity and skill by the six-strong cast – try to discover which is the best sensory experience in their land, they attentively engage individual members of their audience. The children experience the tickle of feathers, and the feel of seeds and water.

Musical and tactile, the production is also superbly visual; not only in the remarkable set, costumes and props (including fabulous seed bowls with light emanating from them), but also in the use of video.

Perhaps the finest of many outstanding moments comes when the children are filmed one by one, before each of them, in turn, has a still image of their face put up on the screen. As the pictures are shown, the cast improvises a song using the child's name as the core lyric.

As I watched the children experience the show, while enjoying the soothing movement ̀ecially-designed hammock chairs, I have no embarrassment in saying I was quite ̀ tears by the enthusiasm, joy and contentment which is achieved by this most ̀ theatre productions.

Audience feedback for *How Long is a Piece of String?* (2008)

Lovely innocent stuff, true (yet simple) 'play' theatre experiences – getting him away from the craziness of certain computer games and visuals on the telly. Superb! Friend and I are big fans, we imagine coming in our fifties (when our two are parents themselves!).

It captured their imagination and involved them from the moment they approached the space. They loved having a role and feeling important. The length was just right. We love your work. It's fantastic. This is our fourth Oily Cart show and it is a complete, absorbing joy for children.

We loved the music and the gentle sense of humour which ran through the show. The attention to detail with the set, costumes and clothing was inspiring and great for the children.

They [the children] were utterly captivated. The performance was so flexible the players were able to accommodate each child's needs. The live music was beautiful, the performers all sang so well and the ambience was so loving, none of us wanted to leave.

Lovely, lovely show. My child (who's four) said, 'I'll really miss that baby,' when he put it back to sleep.

It was very age appropriate – lovely music. Interactive and tactile – especially good for my blind five-year-old.

Parent in Royal National Institute for the Blind Group

It was my great pleasure to accompany my three-year-old granddaughter to your performance while we were visiting London last month. I cannot begin to tell you how much Olivia, her mom, and I enjoyed your amazing performance. As a playwright I learned a great deal about theatre for the very young... a joy for all three generations.

Audience feedback for *Something in the Air* (2009)

The students reacted very well. Amazing reactions to the end songs [which were sung] with their names. Brilliant locating and tracking. Eye contact and listening. Very positive responses!

He was very happy and smiling throughout, which meant he loved it.

Normally she is busy playing with her hands; as she was so interested she stopped.

I'm Joseph's mum, he's five and has learning difficulties and autism. We came to London to see *Something in the Air* at the Unicorn in April. This was one of the most brilliant things we have done with Joseph... so beautifully thought out, with humour, beauty and the greatest of understanding of what works for children like Joseph... oh, and all that lovely swinging and spinning! Singing a special song with each child's name at the end was just lovely. What a brilliant experience for Joseph who really does have a bit of a struggle with life. Thank you. We are big fans and will watch out for the next show.

Although my sons are fidgety, their movements were silent, still and focused, watching what was happening and enjoying the movement and music.

Isaac thoroughly enjoyed the whole experience. We felt looked after from beginning to end. Thank you so much.

The Real Nitty Gritty

The simile which describes an accomplished theatre company as being 'like a swan' – all grace and composure on the surface, but with frantic leg work going on under the water (or, in the case of the theatre company, behind the scenes) – is almost a cliché. But it is absolutely appropriate to Oily Cart. In the following two pieces – by Claire de Loon and Tim Webb – we are given rare insights into how the company's work is enhanced and enabled by the educational, technical and administrative work that is done by the often unsung heroes of theatre making.

Drum 2010

Preparation, anticipation, motivation: before, during and after an Oily Cart show
Claire de Loon

Oily Cart audiences are either very young or have a severe learning disability. Their knowledge of theatre is therefore very limited and an Oily show can be a very frightening prospect for them. We have found that we can help to ease their journey into the imaginative world of the play through various forms of preparation.

Back in 1986, it seemed natural to offer a teachers' resource pack to complement our shows for the very young. We turned to Frances Scott, a highly respected primary school teacher, to help us produce worksheets inspired by *Up on the Roof*. This pack consisted of about twenty photocopied A4 sheets presented in a clear plastic envelope. It contained the story of the show and ideas for activities across the curriculum on the themes of homes and houses. There were drawings of the puppets incorporated into games such as lotto and puzzles.

Frances urged me to assume that the teachers using the pack might be like her – absolutely useless at 'art'. I was to keep the making activities extremely simple and explain them carefully. I know that teachers have many extraordinary skills but they may lack confidence in some areas, like Frances. What they lack most of all is time, so it is important to try to keep the resources simple and practical.

Being a small company without a dedicated education officer, it has always been a struggle for us to produce additional resources in advance of a new show. The extent and form of the resources has varied according to our schedule and funding. However the feedback and obvious results from preparation have been so encouraging that we continue to develop this aspect of the work as a priority.

Ideally we would like the story of an early years show to be as familiar to the children as their favourite books or fairytales. In 1992, we produced a large format illustrated book that told the story of *Greenfingers*, followed by Big Books for *A Peck of Pickled Pepper*, *Perfect Present* and *Roly Poly Pudding*. The obvious thing to complement *A Bit Missing* was a jigsaw puzzle; at the end of the show, the audience were presented with the final piece to complete their puzzle.

At this point, we decided to offer preparatory workshops for children and for teachers. Max and I had a lot of fun going to venues such as Clwyd Theatr Cymru and West Yorkshire *Playhouse* before the show was performed there. We were dressed as jam tarts for *A Peck of Pickled Pepper* (1994) and as posties for *Pass the Parcel* (1998). As part of the games and activities for *Pass the Parcel*, we invited the children to send a letter to someone they loved. They drew beautiful pictures and wrote simple messages to their parents, grandparents or siblings. The teachers accompanying them had been asked to bring the relevant addresses so it was possible for the groups to post their letters on their way home from the theatre. I would love to have seen the excitement when the enchanting letters were opened.

For *Baking Time* (2003), we engaged Fiona Hamilton-Fairley from the Children's Cookery School to help us deliver age-appropriate bakery sessions. The gorgeous smell of bread in the oven and the taste of freshly baked rolls were wonderful.

When we began to make shows for children and young people with severe learning disabilities, we realised that it was essential to provide as much information as possible for their teachers and carers to know what was in store. The shows for children with profound and multiple learning disabilities (PMLD) are complex affairs that require a great deal of liaison with the venues. Schools that have had an Oily Cart show before know to expect disruption and happy upheaval, so the packs are as much for the staff and parents as for the young people.

Our first PMLD educational adviser, Mick Baldwin, an inspired teacher, brainstormed a raft of activities extending the ideas in the show. Mick was not averse to messy play and suggested some great activities involving bottles of paint, which were hilarious. One of our greatest moments involved buckets of *Blue* powder paint, a sheet of clear plastic and a garden hose – on which, more below.

The packs may or may not contain cross-curricular activities, but they always have posters of the characters so that their appearance will be familiar when they arrive.

We also write a social story for the young people on the autistic spectrum. The social story describes concisely what they can expect from the show and it also has simple illustrations showing the characters and the set. It is designed to allay their fears about meeting strangers and being in an unknown environment. It tells them that they can say no if they don't want to participate in a particular activity and it tells them that, at the end of the show, the actors will go away. We usually send both printed and video versions to the schools at least two weeks before the company is due to arrive.

Finally with *Drum* (2011), we started to make a timeline for young people with autistic spectrum disorder. The timeline displays a series of symbols representing the progress of the show from hello to goodbye via feathers, bubbles, rice and so on. It is another tool to help allay anxiety about 'What will happen next?' and 'Where am I in all this?'

It had long been our ambition to embed a character in a school in order to do intense preparation with the pupils. In 2007, this became a reality when Manchester International Festival (MIF) commissioned Oily Cart to perform *Blue* with the addition of two weeks' preparation in two schools. We built a Blues Shack in the courtyard of each school, each containing a Blues person; namely, Boom Boom T (Nicole Worrica) and Pancake Bob (Bob Karper). At first, these Blues People just appeared to be living in the school. They cooked, did their washing, asked the pupils where they could get water or go to the toilet. These informal interactions grew into structured visits to the Blues Shacks where the young people were introduced to the story, characters and songs of *Blue*, along with music and multisensory sessions similar to the ones in the show.

Getting back to the messy play mentioned above, being outside adds a great deal of welcome freedom. The preparatory sessions for *Blue* included 'cookery', making pancakes with lots of flour and breaking eggs, and 'art'. The *Blue* art was still in evidence at one of the schools when we returned two years later. The Blues Shack was still in the courtyard, which remained stained blue all over.

The schools were delighted with the anticipation created through our interventions. When a group from Grange School for autistic young people arrived at the venue, they literally ran into the studio and embraced the actors/

characters they had been hearing about and now finally got to meet. Their teacher was so amazed and delighted that he cried.

MIF enabled us to extend the embedding in 2009, when we performed *Something in the Air* as part of the festival. We put two Nest People in each of three schools for three weeks. The headteacher of Birches School said, 'The children have been really engaged by the Nest People concept. They have loved spending time in the nest and engaging with the Nest People. It has been fantastic to see how positive it has been for children with social, emotional and behavioural difficulties. The nest itself has been a great place for them to visit and to use, and has been a really positive experience to build on children's self-esteem.'

In both *Blue* and *Something in the Air*, we invited the audience to bring an object, which was then integrated into the show. In *Blue*, the characters were waiting for a train to take them home. For this emotional journey, they had Blues Bags that contained their favourite things such as the stars, water, and 'the Groove' (a Blues Person's essence, like their Mojo). We asked the young people to prepare their own Blues Bags. The bags were opened one by one as the characters introduced each young person. The choice of objects in the bags was very personal and revealing. The young people and their carers became fully immersed in the imagined situation and the distinction between characters and audience became blurred. The result was an extremely moving experience of beauty, humour, joy and sadness – a very soulful Blues experience.

In order for *Something in the Air* to begin, the audience had to use the 'red things' they had brought with them to coax the Nest People out of their pods suspended high above our heads. This empowered the young people and, with their humour and spectacular acrobatics, the Ockam's Razor aerialists appeared not as worrying strangers but as gentle, amazing beings to be enjoyed.

Music has always been a fundamental component in every Oily show. So as soon as funds permitted, Max started to record the music of the show. The cassettes and CDs were used as preparation and as a way of reliving the performances after the event. Since 1992's *Dinner Ladies from Outer Space*, all the shows for young people with profound and multiple learning disabilities have had a recording of the music as an essential part of their preparation resources. They are much used by the schools, who have been in touch when their copies have become unusable after being played for years.

Max's scores for the PMLD shows all have a naming song and often a hammocking song. On the recordings there are tracks where the appropriate names can be added by the listeners. The naming songs are sung to individual young people who usually recognise their names and enjoy the heightened personal attention (see *Blue* – The Script). Hammocking is the simplest form of kinaesthetic experience for very disabled young people. It is a technique, which we picked up in a school early on and have built on since, culminating in the epic *Something in the Air*.

When we were researching our first water show, we visited Sue Hewitt, another inspirational teacher, at William Morris School. She introduced us to the idea of using different moods of music to accompany multisensory sessions. The music of the show has often contained tracks accompanied by suggestions on how to use the different passages for a multisensory session made either by a voice-over or a printed sheet.

In 2002 we created *Jumpin' Beans*, an early years show in three versions for ages six months to two years, two to four and four to six-year-olds. Our educational advisor was Hazel Davies, a specialist in movement for early years. Hazel devised sessions to be used by carers using the booklet accompanying the CD. Ever since then, recording the music has become a part of the rehearsal period for all our shows.

New technology has enabled us to reach more people more effectively. We can put resources such as the social stories online so that every teacher in a school or a parent at home can download them immediately. Our IT guru, Nick Weldin, has kept us up to date with all the latest developments that increase accessibility for all our audiences but in particular those with severe intellectual impairments. Nick created an elaborate interactive website for *Something in the Air*. He visited the schools as a Nest Person to help them to make full use of this exciting resource. More recently, our great advisor for audiences with complex learning disabilities, Richard Burbage, inspired Nick and me to make an interactive social story for *Gorgeous*. Still images, text and recorded voice could be projected onto a screen or classroom whiteboard and the pupils could click on them to trigger video of the characters introducing themselves.

We have used many techniques over the years to enhance the audience's experience of our shows. We have had success in building up anticipation and in keeping the memory of the experience alive. The creation of the shows and maintaining their quality is our primary goal but we appreciate that whenever possible, it is rewarding to enrich the shows with the additional resources.

I would like to end with some feedback about *Ring a Ding Ding* from Catherine Davies, class teacher and early years co-ordinator at Michael Faraday Primary School in South London. You couldn't ask for a better illustration of how an Oily show has motivated children to use their imagination and explore ideas introduced in the play:

> My nursery classes who attended on 6/7 December (2011) have carried on the show with them going 'round and round and round' on our bikes and tricycles, drawing circles everywhere, looking for circles and spheres everywhere, making puppets, being Alice and her dog, playing chime bars and drums along to the CD, singing the songs, talking about the Earth and the sun etc, etc.

Oily Biz: the business side of Oily Cart
Tim Webb

Usually when I am giving a talk or leading a workshop about Oily Cart, people want me to concentrate on the art, and what makes it possible. I like to suggest the art of the Cart comes to me in a vision as I sit in my Istanbul penthouse sucking a shisha pipe. Unfortunately nothing in the preceding sentence is true. Elsewhere I have described the process by which the Oily Cart team put a new show together, but I left out any evaluation of the essential role played on our work by the board, the general managers and the administrators of the company. What follows is not just a courteous thank you to the people behind the scenes without whom ... etc. It is an attempt to describe the work of the people who provide the political, financial and logistical structure of the organisation, and without whom there would be no Oily Cart shows.

To begin at the beginning. It was great back in the day. Just the two of us, Max Reinhardt and myself, on the road in a rusty Renault. There was no company structure. No board. No overheads. No money. Ah, the early eighties! Mrs Thatcher; the Falklands War; the miners' Strike; the dismembering of British industry. Our salad days!

Then things got more serious. In 1984 we received a grant from the Greater London Council, before Mrs Thatcher dismembered that too. Then, after seven years of project grants in 1990 the Arts Council of Great Britain gave us our first chunk of revenue funding, covering some of our core costs. It came in the nick of time. The Arts Council had turned down our revenue application the year before and we were on the point of packing it in and getting proper jobs.

Up to this time Max had taken care of the bulk of the company admin, but the coming of the revenue money required that we become a charity and form ourselves into a company limited by guarantee. To be a company meant that we had to have a Board of Trustees and we were very fortunate in the individuals that we invited onto that first board. Our very first chair, Jeff Teare – at that time an associate director at Theatre Royal, Stratford East – was very influential as the board took its first steps. Being a director himself, Jeff was determined that art should be left to the artists as much as possible. This meant that he suppressed discussion of Oily Cart shows at board level, mostly restricting it to a few jaundiced comments of his own about our latest production.

Sarah Holmes, then in charge of marketing at Stratford East (and currently chief executive at the New Wolsey Theatre, Ipswich), was another great influence during the first few years of the board's life. She encouraged us in the company to take the role of the board seriously and to see how board members could help by keeping a critical but supportive eye on the work while, for the most part, leaving the people actually creating the shows to make the key artistic decisions.

We've had the support of a succession of strong boards over the years, and they've helped us through a number of potential crises. I've served as trustee for several other arts organisations and have seen the shenanigans that can arise at board level – for example, decisions being taken over policy while the artists who will have to deliver that policy are asked to leave the room. Very different from Oily Cart board meetings, which are, mostly, models of informed and objective support given by board members motivated by the desire to get the company to deliver the best theatre possible.

Our long-serving chairs Tim James, Brian Harris, Arti Prashar and the present incumbent, Lisa Mead, have all provided invaluable support at points when the going got rough. A notable feature of the Oily Cart is the presence at all our board meetings of our auditors. Sometimes it will be Jon Catty, sometimes Bridget Kalloushi, not infrequently both. Their advice is invariably worth listening to and on more than one occasion they have steered us away from potential disaster.

Apart from a strong board, the other essential for a theatre company is a really good general manager. The Oily Cart general manager has the responsibility for preparing the budgets and for fundraising from all sources, as well being in charge of the overall organisation and financial management of the company including marketing and personnel. The Oily Cart is very dependent on the support of Arts Council England, and the general manager takes the lead in all negotiations with them as she does with the trusts and foundations that do so much to support our work for young people with a learning disability. The truth is that but for our general managers the Oily Cart might never have got much past its 'two men in a rusty Renault' phase.

Our first, full-time general manager, Joanna Ridout, put the company on its financial feet and began the serious fundraising to support our theatre for people with a learning disability. Rebecca Farrar, our general manager for eight years, began the negotiations that resulted in us gaining a long lease on our Smallwood School premises, as well as the fundraising to enable us to make the building fully accessible and fit for purpose. The indispensible Kathy Everett, our current general manager, has also devoted a great deal of her time at Oily Cart to the business of securing the lease on, and advancing the development of, the premises. In addition, she has proved to be one of the all-time-great fundraisers, and is noted for deftly producing pieces of paper containing incontestable statistics at key points in negotiations.

Second-in-line to the general manager is the Oily Cart administrator who takes responsibility for booking tours and accommodation and transport. Our current administrator, Alison Garratt, also has a major part to play in our marketing, maintaining the database, updating the website, minuting meetings and being the first point of contact for those who call or visit the company. She is the one who deals with a daily avalanche of enquiries about the company from students around the world. Another taxing part of her job is having to explain to Special Needs schools that would like to book one of our shows that our work for these audiences is oversubscribed nine times over. The waiting times for schools outside our local borough of Wandworth in London is long and some will have to wait for a year or more before an Oily Cart visit is possible.

Alison is already proving a worthy successor to fabulous administrators from the company's past, now gone on to greater things – people like Emily Brown, Kevin Walsh and Sarah Crompton. Heartfelt thanks are due to Roger Lang who took administrative control of the company on the two occasions when Kathy Everett was on maternity leave. Roger was at the controls during much of the testing period when we redeveloped our Smallwood premises and was also responsible for the myriad of negotiations connected with the publication of the book you are now holding.

Of course, we are also indebted to a host of people working for other organisations. Max and I would surely still be stuck in that Renault, without the programmers and producers who book our shows, the Arts Council England officers who have helped support us over the years and the officers and the trustees of the charitable organisations who have backed our efforts to take great theatre to audiences for whom there is often little alternative provision.

So, when I'm asked what it takes to get a theatre company off the ground and to keep it flying, I'm afraid the answer is complicated. A successful theatre company requires artistic skills and it certainly needs a vision, but without people looking after the business side of things it will never flourish. Arts managers and administrators are rarely celebrated like the performers out there in the spotlight, but they are indispensible. They have provided the means by which we translate our dreams into action. No theatre company is possible without people like them.

Afterword
Mark Brown

It was in 2008 that I realised just how much I love Oily Cart Theatre Company. My sister-in-law Lindsey, my nephew Rory, who was then three years old and I had just come out of the magical, stringy, ropey world of *How Long is a Piece of String?*, which the company had performed at the wonderfully child-centred MacRobert Arts Centre at the University of Stirling.

As we got into the car and Lindsey was buckling Rory into his child seat, I noticed the cast of the show getting into the Oily Cart van, which was parked in front of my car. As the van started to reverse, I said jokingly, to Lindsey, 'Wouldn't it be funny if Oily Cart reversed their van into the critic's...', THUMP, 'car?!'

The alarmed and embarrassed actors came running round to check that no harm had been done to people or vehicle (none had), and I laughingly repeated to them what I had been in the midst of saying at the moment of impact. I doubt very much that I would have taken the little episode so well had the people in the van not just provided my loved ones and me with such a brilliantly conceived and beautifully performed piece of promenade theatre. That's the thing about Oily Cart, they may not be much cop at reversing vans but they make bloody good shows.

It is, perhaps, no coincidence that I, as a Scottish theatre critic, should have come to edit this book. Not only did the Oily Cart story begin in my home city of Glasgow when Tim Webb and Claire de Loon met at the Citizens Theatre in 1971, but Scotland has in recent times achieved real excellence where children's theatre is concerned. The MacRobert Arts Centre is a top class venue for children's work, one that Tim Webb believes is among the very best in the UK. The Imaginate Children's International Theatre Festival, which is held each spring in Edinburgh, is Britain's biggest showcase of children's theatre.

Crucially, Scottish children's theatre has – thanks to companies such as Catherine Wheels and Wee Stories, artists like Andy Manley and Shona Reppe, and projects such as Starcatchers – achieved a deservedly proud place in the country's culture.

In my 18 years as a theatre critic, I have had the great pleasure of seeing high quality work for children from across Scotland, the UK and the world. Of all that diverse, imaginative, hilarious and poignant work, however, the greatest children's theatre company I have so far encountered is without doubt Oily Cart.

Other artists interact with their child audience, but none engage children so thoroughly in the development of the story, whether it is in sensory, physical or vocal terms. Other artists make exquisite sets, costumes and props but no-one achieves the beautiful balance between sumptuousness and theatrical practicality of Oily Cart. Other artists weave lovely live and recorded music into their productions but no-one can match the Oilies' cleverly conceptually attuned music or their by turns touching and hilariously silly lyrics.

No other children's theatre company I have seen offers such diverse casts of truly remarkable performers. For example, to see Griff Fender taking the mickey out of himself in one of his many astonishingly stupid roles is to see an actor as a master of his craft and in perfect tune with all generations of his broad audience.

The glory of Oily Cart's work – as is clear both in the contributions to this book made by the three members of the creative core themselves, and in the observations others make of their shows – is that it is in the most meaningful sense total theatre. Over their three decades in the outrageously neglected sectors in which they work, Oily Cart have carefully honed their processes and aesthetics, and established tried and tested techniques in everything from the use of colour to cast recruitment and audition to the point where every show achieves a near perfect match between concept, cast, performance, design, music and technical execution.

Take, for instance, *Ring a Ding Ding*. As explored earlier in this volume, every aspect of this show – from the narrative, to the set design, the music, and the movement of both the actors and audience – was consistent with the central concepts of ringing and circularity. The southern African-style wire puppets in the show were made with recycled materials, recycling being a form of circularity. The music was built around the ringing sounds of bells. When the audience wasn't turning round the turntable upon which the puppets moved, they were on their feet, walking round the circular set, while a musician cycled round and round on a tricycle. And from a dog who chases his own tail to a crazy ship's captain who sails his boat on endless circular trips around the bay, the story itself was built around characters who go round in circles.

Such conceptual consistency and attention to detail are typical of Oily Cart's work. Add these qualities to a professionalism which is as rigorous as it is good humoured, a superb understanding of their target audiences, gained through hands-on experience in performance as much as through careful research, and a high degree of organised freedom for performers, and you have a very powerful theatrical combination.

The basis of all of this is fundamentally political. Oily Cart are, in the broadest sense of the word, humanists. They are humanists in the same sense that the surrealist humorist, poet and songwriter Ivor Cutler was a humanist; indeed, Cutler adored children and they reciprocated that adoration in their appreciation of his work.

Like Cutler, the Oilies have always allowed themselves tremendously silly flights of fancy. One need only look at the titles of some of the earliest Oily Cart shows – *Beam Us Up Spotty, Parrots of Penzance, Slipped Disco* – to see that this is a company that from its very inception rejected the patronising idea that theatre for children had to be narrowly educational and morally instructive.

The Oilies made the politically and socially progressive observation that young children and children and young people with learning disabilities were terribly neglected audiences. To then conclude that those audiences deserved a high quality theatre of joyful entertainment and multisensory pleasure at least as much as any other audience was more progressive still.

It comes as little surprise to learn in Tim Webb's preceding piece on the business side of Oily Cart, that in 1984 Oily Cart received a grant from the Greater London Council. The Cart's progressive agenda of creating high quality theatre for socially marginalised audiences fitted with the attempts by the GLC – so hated by Thatcherism – to bring the arts to sections of society who were previously peripheral to arts planning, if they were considered by it at all.

Much is said nowadays by both politicians and the arts funding organisations who direct arts funding on their behalf about 'social inclusion'. However, the realities of arts policy and funding often lead to justified scepticism that this is a mere buzz phrase, leading to a tokenistic tick box approach that prizes the pursuit of targets ('How many disabled children did you perform to?', 'Did your work promote healthier lifestyles?') over artistic quality.

The beauty of Oily Cart's work is that it stands resolutely against tokenism and in favour of artistic quality. I have to confess, when I arranged to see my first Oily Cart show, one which was designed for children and young people with very profound learning disabilities, I was, I'm ashamed to say, unaware of the company's tremendous reputation. I went to the MacBob fearing that I would encounter a piece of theatre that was well-meaning, worthy, but ultimately unremarkable. What I encountered instead was a visually gorgeous, beautifully performed, technically accomplished, lyrical and poetic theatre piece inspired by the great Persian book of poems entitled *The Conference of the Birds*.

Far from being well-intentioned amateurs filling a vacuum in theatre provision for a neglected audience, it was obvious within seconds of the performance beginning that Oily Cart were working at the very highest level. Every element of the piece was as accomplished as the others. Each aspect of the play, from the costumes to the music, showed its subtle Persian influences.

Nowhere was the tremendous professionalism of the show reflected more than in the work of the performers themselves, whose capacity to create a wonderfully benign environment for their young audience and to sustain that atmosphere communicatively both in spoken word and beautifully sung song caught me quite by surprise. As the joy of the children showed on their faces, I was – as I wrote in my review at the time and am happy to repeat here – unashamedly moved to tears.

The evolution of Oily Cart's total theatre is testament not only to the company's founding principles, particularly its artistic integrity and progressive political outlook, but also to its capacity to adapt and set itself new challenges. Who would have thought, back in 1981 when Tim and Max started out in the old Renault, that by 2009 they would be collaborating with a company of aerial artists on *Something in the Air*? Or that in 2012 they would be working with the Royal Shakespeare Company on *In a Pickle*, a children's show inspired by the Bard's play *The Winter's Tale*?

It is of course absurd that children's theatre should be considered the Cinderella of stage work. Far from being easier to make than theatre for adults, children's theatre has to take account of children's rapid journey through various stages of development and is consequently more difficult to create. Making work for children and young people with often profound and multiple learning disabilities is a greater challenge still. The fact that Oily Cart make it look so easy is perhaps the greatest tribute to their brilliance.

In the course of 18 years as a theatre critic one sees the work of hundreds, perhaps thousands, of theatre companies. Only a few leave an indelible mark on one's mind. Since my first encounter with their work in 2005, Oily Cart has been one of those companies for me. My admiration of their work has grown with every show I have seen and every encounter I have had with Tim, Claire, Max and members of the various casts.

I consider it a great honour to have been invited to bring together this volume celebrating 30 years of their remarkable work. Long may the Oily Cart make its unique and wonderful way through the lives of young audiences.

Glasgow
May 2012

Also from Trentham Books

Theatre for Young Audiences
a critical handbook
edited by Tom Maguire and Karian Schuitema

This exciting book is designed to develop an academic and critical understanding of children's theatre today.

Literature on this aspect of children's theatre is surprisingly sparse, when so much writing, creating and performing is going on in the UK, making accessible and original work of excellent artistic quality specifically for the young. Some follow the tradition of adapting children's literature into theatrical performances which incorporate puppetry, dance and live music; others reflect the numerous cultural influences in the UK and represent them on stage.

Some of the best and most innovative of such work is analysed in this book. The contributors include Gill Brigg, David Broster, Dominic Hingorani, Jeanne Klein, Geoffrey Readman, Matthew Reason, James Reynolds, Peter Wynne-Wilson, Jan Wozniak and Oily Cart's Tim Webb.

Dr Tom Maguire is Senior Lecturer in the School of Creative Arts at University of Ulster. Karian Schuitema has created the Children's Theatre in the UK Research Network and is completing her PhD at University of Westminster.

September 2012, ISBN 978 1 85856 501 9
172 pages, 244 x 170mm, £24.99

www.trentham-books.co.uk